GILBERT WALTER LYTTELTON TALBOT

Edited by Paul Foster, FRSA

Published by Minutecircle Services Limited

ISBN 978-1-908345-08-0

© *Paul Foster*

All rights reserved. No part of this publication may be reproduced, stored in a retrieval system, or transmitted in any form or by any means, electronic, mechanical, photocopying, recording or otherwise without either the prior written permission of the Publishers or a licence permitting restricted copying issued by the UK Copyright Service, 4 Tavistock Avenue, Didcot, Oxfordshire OX11 8NA.

Design and typesetting by Minutecircle Limited, 12 Conqueror Court, Sittingbourne, Kent ME10 5BH.

*This book is dedicated to my lifelong friends
Chris and Sheila Buckwell*

*In memory of my grandfather
Sergeant Frank Heesom
1893 - 1974*

Gilbert Walter Lyttelton Talbot

Born September 1, 1891. Killed in Action at Hooge, July 30, 1915

"And your bright Promise . . .
Is touched, stirs, rises, opens, and grows sweet
And blossoms and is you, when you are dead."

By the Same Author

Other Books In The "I Was There!" Series:

A Memoir, Edward Wyndham Tennant

Active-Service Diary (Lieutenant E H Shears, Irish Guards)

Attack, an infantry subaltern's impression of July 1st 1916 (E G D Liveing)

Denis Oliver Barnett, In Happy Memory (his letters from France and Flanders, October 1915 — August 1915)

Gilbert Walter Lyttelton Talbot

Julian Grenfell and Francis & Riversdale Grenfell - A Memoir

Letters by Captain Sir Edward Hulse, Bt, 2nd Battalion Scots Guards

Letters from Flanders by A D Gillespie

Letters of Lieutenant Colonel George Laurie, November 4th 1914-March 11th 1915

Letters to his Wife - R E Vernède

Richard Vincent Sutton, a record of his life together with extracts from his private papers

Soldier and Dramatist, being the letters of Harold Chapin

The Letters of Arthur George Heath

Charles Lister - Letters & Recollections

visit: www.remembering1418.com

GILBERT WALTER LYTTELTON TALBOT

Editor's Introduction

Gilbert was born at home on Tuesday 1st September 1891 when his father was Vicar of Leeds. He was the youngest son of The Right Reverend Edward Stuart Talbot and the Honourable Mrs Lavinia Talbot. He was educated at Winchester College and went up to Christ Church, Oxford, where became the President of the Union.

It was clear that Gilbert was to make a career in politics and it was considered by many that he would have at least become a member of the Cabinet, if not appointed as Prime Minister. The First World War was to destroy his potential and end his life, one amongst so many.

Gilbert's name lives on in Poperinghe at *'Talbot House'*, part of the TOC H organisation. I hope that the many visitors The Ypres Salient, and particularly to *'Talbot House'*, will find this publication of interest and provide an insight into the man who inspired so many.

Gilbert's parents produced the main body of this book in his memory in 1917 as a private publication. I have faithfully reproduced the text of the book, the emphasis given in the original has been maintained, however, the footnotes are now incorporated within the narrative in brackets. I have added, where appropriate, contemporary illustrations and photographs — these are my personal choice to help the enjoyment of the text. The photographs of Gilbert are placed in the same position within the book as the original.

The second part contains additional information and cameos on many of the events and those who were mentioned in the original publication.

I hope that you enjoy reading the insight to Gilbert's life as much I have.

Contents

Editor's Introduction	7
Contents	8 - 10
Original Introductions	11 - 12
Boyhood	13 - 17
Winchester	18 - 19
Oxford	20 - 27
Home	28
Religion	29 - 30
The War	31 - 36
Diary From The Front	37 - 48
Reflections on Ypres by Lieutenant Colonel Butler and Lieutenant Jones	44
Last Letters	49 - 51
Canon Scott Holland Memoir	51 - 56
Appendix	
I The Fighting At Hooge In The Last Days Of July 1915	
From John Buchan's 'History of the War'	59 - 60
Sergeant Chumley's Account	60 - 61
Private Nash's Account	61 - 62
B/3484 Rifleman G H Nash, DCM	62
II Extracts From Letters Of Gilbert's Friends	63 - 71
III A Few Contributions Of His Own	72 - 80
Notes on 'RMS Titanic'	73

Part II

Sanctuary Wood Cemetery
    Cemetery details from the CWGC   82
    Plan of the cemetery   83
    Lieutenant Gilbert Talbot's grave   84 - 85

Some Members of Gilbert's Family
    His father, Edward Stuart Talbot   86 - 87
    His Siblings:
    Mary Catherine Talbot   87
    Edward Keble Talbot   87
    Nevile Stuart Talbot   87
    His Uncle, General Sir Nevile Lyttelton, GCB, GCVO, PC   87 - 88
    His Cousin, Mary Hermione Lyttelton, CBE   88

From Training To Burial   89 - 91

Officers Of The Battalion Who Died The Same Day Include
    2nd Lieutenant Guy Devitt   92 - 93
    Lieutenant John Fosdick   93
    2nd Lieutenant Alan Godsal   94
    2nd Lieutenant Frederick Marriott   95 - 96

The 8th Rifle Brigade At Hooge and 'Liquid Fire'   97 - 101

Some Of The Awards Won By The Rifle Brigade On 30th July 1915   102 - 103

Those Mentioned in the Text
    Lieutenant Raymond Asquith   105 - 108
    Arthur Balfour, KG, OM, PC, DL   109
    2nd Lieutenant Eric Benison   109
    Hubert Burge, Bishop of Southwark   110
    Captain Spencer Drummond   110 - 111
    2nd Lieutenant The Hon Billy Grenfell   111 - 114
    'Into Battle' by Julian Grenfell   112
    Captain Ronald Hardy   114 - 115
    Colonel James Heriot-Maitland, CMG, DSO   115
    Canon Henry Holland   116
    General Sir Archibald Hunter, GCB, GCVO, DSO   117 - 118
    Captain The Hon Edward Kay-Shuttleworth   118 - 120
    The Most Reverend and Rt Hon Baron Lang, GCVO, PC, DD   120 - 121
    David Lloyd-George   121

GILBERT WALTER LYTTELTON TALBOT

Lieutenant Ian Macandrew	122
Brigadier General Ronald Maclachlan, DSO	123 - 124
John Gordon Swift MacNeill, KC, MP	124
Walter Monckton, 1st Viscount Monckton, GCVO, KCMG	125
2nd Lieutenant Thomas Rae	125 - 126
2nd Lieutenant Sidney Woodroffe, VC	127 - 128
TOC H and 'Tubby' Clayton	129
IC&GM Battlefield Tours	132

GILBERT WALTER LYTTELTON TALBOT

This little book was privately printed, and given to a large number of my son's school and Oxford friends, and to his comrades, officers and men.

There was no thought of publication. But requests from strangers, or from those who wished to give it to others, and the words written and spoken about it have led us to think that it might have its word to say to some for whom he was only a name.

If this hope should be fulfilled, and if, in particular, his life, with its hopes and aspirations, should help to rouse or encourage any of the younger ones on whom will fall, after the War, the tasks and battles of peace, nothing could bring us more true comfort.

EDW. WINTON.
November 1916.

GILBERT WALTER LYTTELTON TALBOT

Words written by way of introduction when the little book was first privately printed. — E. W.

IT seemed to us right to preserve some account of a short life which, as we knew, had given light and warmth to not a few while he was with us here: and had been thought to show promise of future distinction.

Crowned with honour by the manner of its passing from this present world, it may still give out, even here for a while, some light of example and encouragement.

With this hope, as well as with the love which will not willingly let memory pass, even in *'this transitory life'*, the little memoir is printed.

It has been put together by his Mother. To the many friends whose words enrich it we are truly grateful.

May God be with it — and with him.

EDW. WINTON.

FARNHAM CASTLE
June 1916.

GILBERT TALBOT

It was the liveliest, merriest little fellow that was born in the Vicarage of Leeds on 1 September 1891. The high spirits and abounding vitality which were Gilbert's — owing no doubt a good deal to his splendid health — gave a great charm and delight to his short life.

He very early showed one characteristic a vivid knowledge of what he wanted, with an equally vivid insistence and ingenuity in securing it, delighting in the little plans and arrangements which triumphed over difficulties. Being a good deal the youngest of his family, he was more in the position of an only child, especially in his nursery days, and it was a disadvantage to his natural tendency to think rather too much of Number One that no one stood in his way or snatched away his toys. The many infectious illnesses which were his portion were perhaps not unwholesome times of discipline in his little radiant days — not that he emerged from them at all impaired in health, but he had to forgo many happy hours in little gay flittings over the house, welcomed every- where with his sunny smile and insinuating ways. When at about six he had measles, followed rather quickly by scarlet fever, he sent me a message through his nurse — *"It is hard that I should have measles and scarlet fever, when I am so happy downstairs!"* At all times he was full of life and spring, running about from morning to night, very rarely walking.

A row of ugly dolls at one time took the place of companions. They were given odd names — 'Fruit', 'Busgwy', etc. — and games and plots centred round them with lively imagination. But nothing charmed him anything like so much as the fairy tales of the nursery — Grimm in particular — and all the old-fashioned nursery rhymes. When a much-enduring Miss Rosenberg endeavoured to get him quiet for sitting for a miniature when he was about four, the only hope was for one of us to begin 'This is the House that Jack built', and so on, through pages of what he knew every word by heart. A little later he knew in the same way the life of Joan of Arc and the history of the old Rochester Tower, etc. One of his great joys at this time was in going any little excursion with his father or me. He went with his father to the 'Zoo', and was more full of it afterwards than at the time. Perhaps he was rather subdued by the unexpected hollow roar of the lions, when awaiting their food. His little hand tightened in his father's, and he said, "Shall we have a little fresh air!" Like so many boys — only showing it more — he could not bear being beaten in games, and even at eight or nine there might be a downpour of tears at a defeat. On my remonstrances on this baby habit over lawn-tennis, etc., he said cheerfully, *"Well, I've left off crying in cricket!"* He was very plucky in learning to swim at St. David's, Reigate, and used to jump off a high plank into the arms of a big brother or sister, in the great swimming bath of the School, one summer holiday.

Gilbert was devoted to Uty from baby days. ['Uty *'was the pet name of Gilbert's nurse, Mrs. Finch, to whom he was devoted from the first year of his life till the last, and* who has now been thirty-six years in the family.] With her nursing, her reading aloud — which all the children delighted in — her talk and her games, she kept the little nursery alive. Years later, when he was reading for 'Greats', he used to get her to sit opposite him, reading a translation of Herodotus at a little table on the terrace at Farnham, while he took notes from the text. He would be delighted at finding himself alone with her sometimes at home: "Better company you couldn't have", he used to say. He arranged several visits for her to Winchester and Oxford, and she always came with us till quite lately on our summer holidays. [*Once she travelled with Gilbert to Switzerland when he was a small boy, to join us there. At Paris all the chaff and coaxing in the world failed to dislodge her from her firm position on her boxes to go outside the station to get some dinner. With much suspicion of foreign food, and anxiety over the boxes, Uty remained where she was; on which Gilbert made his way to a little restaurant close by, and brought off a very satisfactory French dinner for himself.*]

There was something magnetic and with the spirit of a leader about him always. Many guests who only saw him in one visit to Kennington remember him well, and can recall the vivid, keen little figure, not a bit shy, taking them to see the house and chapel, giving them any information he could, and always full of spirits and merriment — and politics! To a fault, however, he was insistent on claiming attention and in having his say in and out of season, and in arranging and ordering things as he wished.

He was fond of talking of his *'big brothers'*, and would describe the games, etc., he would have with them in their holidays. His affection for and belief in his two brothers was very marked always, and he eagerly wanted his special friends to know them. With Ted the tie of both being Wykehamists was very close, and there was endless chaff and fun between them, and I have often heard Gilbert say that *"Ted was one of the best arguers he knew"*.

Two friends write of his boyhood:

"All we remember of those happy holidays at Timberscombe twelve years ago radiates happiness and exuberant vitality. It is difficult to think of him without a smile."

"Timberscombe, a village on Exmoor, was that 'time of his life 'when he learnt to ride well and fearlessly with the staghounds, being small enough to ride an Exmoor pony no one else could share with him!"

And another writer after a visit to Bishop's House:

"He was such an attractive, brilliant, generous boy, I shall never forget my first sight of him at Kennington — suspensum loculos — just off to school, and saying good-bye round the breakfast table, like a young collie, fresh and bustling and handsome'.

Two or three almost passionate instincts in him revealed themselves very early — love of fun and nonsense, and love of beauty. He would repeat the whole of *'Dame Wiggins of Lee'*, the old-fashioned humorous poem, with embellishments of his own, and a little later on it was page after page of *'Uncle Remus '*(Brer Rabbit), which he poured forth with shining eyes and clear utterance, till we had to cry for mercy. *'Punch '*he had a very early appreciation of, and one of his constant habits through his life was to pick out the bits in the letterpress which he felt sure would specially amuse me, and we have often laughed together till we have cried over many a choice bit.

And then the love of beauty. The sound of his own voice reciting bits of Tennyson, Wordsworth, and many others, must have been delightful to him, and made him keen to impress their beauty on others by constantly repeating his favourite lines. May [*His eldest sister.*] taught him most of his poetry. When so small a boy that he had to stand on a high foot-stool to be properly seen, in a large crowded room, he asked if he might recite to the newly-ordained men on an Ordination Sunday afternoon at Kennington. One of his pieces was '*Young Lochinvar*', another '*Up the airy mountain, down the rushy glen*', and the beautiful poem of Wordsworth, '*I wandered lonely as a cloud*'. It was comic to see the little man, with his baby face and sparkling blue eyes, give out with great feeling and clearness:

> *And oft when on my couch I lie,*
> *In vacant or in pensive mood,*
> *They flash upon that inward eye,*
> *Which is the bliss of solitude.*

Closely associated with his love of beautiful language was his love of music. During part of our life in London he was immensely occupied with a great enthusiasm for the choir of the Cathedral Church of Southwark, then in the charge of a very talented organist, Dr. Madeley Richardson. The personal friendship with him and his keen following of all his musical views interested and absorbed him, and during many holidays he would be at the afternoon weekly service as often as possible — besides Sundays — getting to know the whole choir personally, as well as entering into the music — the anthems, the 'masses' for choral celebration and especially the Psalms. Dr. Richardson had written music for the whole Psalter, drawing out the meanings of the words with extreme care. Gilbert's great love of beauty and of melody in music and in words made him enter very keenly into this musical-dramatic interpretation of the Psalms.

Dr. Richardson has sent me the following words about their time together: "*Some of the happiest memories of my life are connected with dear Gilbert's association with Southwark Cathedral, beginning when a lad of ten years old. ... After some singing lessons from myself, his interest in his own singing passed on to what I was doing at the Cathedral. He began coming to sit with me on the organ seat during the services, when he would take pleasure in finding the places in my music books, starting the water power and helping in other ways, evidently liking to feel that he had some active part in contributing to the general result. Then later he began to attend the choir practices, and came more and more frequently.*

He gradually became quite absorbed in the Cathedral music and the work of the choir. He appeared to apply all his mind to it, and acquired a considerable knowledge unusual in one so young. I was sometimes surprised to find how much he really knew about Church music; and he would say things that showed sound judgment and taste. His interest in the personnel of the choir, and especially of the boys, was very strong. . . .

When he went to Winchester I thought that perhaps the new life and associations would lessen his interest in the Cathedral music. But it seemed to make no difference. On returning home he would come straight to the Cathedral, to his old place at the organ. ..."

This marked love of beauty, whether of poetry and beautiful things, of buildings in lovely surroundings, such as Winchester and Oxford, or of mountain, coast, or home scenery — as at the Chalet des Melezes, S. Gervais les Bains, [*Twice Gilbert joined a Reading Party with Mr. Urquhart, Fellow of Balliol, at the Chalet.*] Harlech, Falconhurst, etc. — gave a thread of romance to all Gilbert's life and was at the bottom of his extreme delight in living at Farnham his last four years. London meant, of course, so much to him of keen enjoyment, social and political, with his immense delight in plays, that I could scarcely believe the change to Farnham at nineteen would have been so happy a one. I cannot recall one word of regret for the *'flesh pots'* of London, once we began to live at Farnham. The place took the strongest hold of him, and he was swept away by the hot, radiant beauty of the summer of 1911, when many of his friends came and enjoyed it all with him. I remember on turning into Castle Street one day, coming home, he said quite passionately to me: *'Mother, you adore Farnham, don't you, as I do, when we come in sight of it like this — each time?'* And then the skilful and anxious work of the repairing of the Keep, in 1913-14, the glory of the flowers and flowering shrubs, the distant views and the great cool spaces in the summer time were a constant delight. Of Christmas Eve 1911 at Farnham he wrote: "... *We had rather a pretty little show here last night. My eldest brother was made up as Father Christmas, and the nephews with a few other children waited for him at the drawing room window. He came round the moat, by the old wall of the castle, carrying a lantern: the effect was really charming, and the children completely deceived. Richard in my arms became like a little fire football with quite delirious excitement, mingled with a touch of terror at the first sight of him. He came in and gave presents all round, and talked a lot most cleverly to the children, and then disappeared again into the garden and away round the moat. It was all quite fascinating.*

Meanwhile May did her best to convey to her children the theological significance of Christmas, the main result being that her second son asked whether *'God came down from Heaven by a rope, and if so did he hold on very tight?"*

In March 1912, again: "... *This morning is a perfect spring day, though a little windy. I'm absolutely knocked down by the beauty of the place. It's almost too good to be true. Everything is fresh and green and budding with the promise of spring in the air, grass, flowers, trees and everything else. The daffodils, hyacinths, violets and heaps of brilliant spring flowers are everywhere in the garden and among the rocks of the keep. The top of the keep is really a sort of Paradise. I've never seen it all look so beautiful as after breakfast this morning, the sun flooding the whole place, and with that extraordinary feeling of vigour and youth and beauty which is never quite so good at any other time of the year. ..."*

And of his last sight of the place he wrote on 19 May 1915: "... *I went to Farnham for the last time in the afternoon. The place never looked more lovely, flooded with sunshine, and the blossoms and wallflowers in full blaze. I wandered round it all with Uty and the dogs. . . . May I see it all again soon! ..."*

London, it must be said, kept one great charm for him in the fact of the beautiful Governor's House at Chelsea being in his Uncle Neville's hands. It was a second home to him; he was often visiting there. And he was an enthusiastic playgoer, with an intimate knowledge of all that world of theatres and London music halls — not easily shocked by plays or novels. But he vehemently drew the line at the last half of the second volume of *'sinister Street'*: *"I shouldn't like to think of any girl or woman I know reading it"*.

When Gilbert was about eight years old the South African War broke out. His interest in it knew no bounds. The fact that Neville, already in the 1st Battalion of the Rifle Brigade, was going out of course gave it at once a personal interest. When Neville started from home in September 1899, the small brother squeezed a hot shilling into his hand as he was getting into the cab. During the early and exciting period of the war there was no detail Gilbert missed. He could have stood a cross-examination in all the battles, small or big, and in the generals and heroes on the Natal side of the fighting. He got hold of the newspapers the moment they came into the house, and guests were disturbed now and again by his running through the passages with the dinner bell, shouting out the news of an insignificant victory. He and Oliver (son of his uncle Alfred Lyttelton) shared classes together in Great College Street (and later went together to Mr. Bull's private school in Marylebone), and both enjoyed doing endless military things together and playing the war in games. But it never became a question with either of them of going into the army till the call came in August 1914.

In September 1905 Gilbert went to Winchester to the house of Mr. Bramston (known to all Wykehamists as *'Trant'*). His eldest brother, Edward (himself a keen Wykehamist), took him there, in the absence of his father abroad. He writes the following sketch of the six years at Winchester:

"Never did a boy (he was barely 13) enter a public school with a lighter heart than Gilbert. I can see him now on that first day, as I left him to buy his experience. His untidy clothes and a free and easy manner to new acquaintances betrayed no sign of apprehension or self-consciousness; and he was full of talk on various subjects till the last moment."

He was in those early days, I make no doubt, a fit object of the suspicion which schoolboys have for one who *'jaws'*, and who assumes that he can treat with those older than himself on equal terms. Indeed, Gilbert's first year and half at Winchester contained much adversity and even misery. Much of the fault was his. He was too self-confident and assertive, and did not take pains enough with his *'sweating'* duties. But even this period was ennobled by a deep shrinking from uncleanness and by the isolation which resistance to it brought upon him.

It speaks well for the good-will of his House and for Gilbert's courage that he started so soon on the happiness which steadily grew through the following years. The spell of Trant's broad and lovable humanity, which has charmed so many generations of Wykehamists, won all Gilbert's warm and loyal affection. To critics of Trant's system, he used to reply that Trant was his own system, and in that fact he found compensation for some of the early troubles to which, perhaps, a certain lack of discipline contributed. He became one of the most devoted Wykehamists, passionately enthusiastic over the school and his years there. *"Every minute is precious and every stone a jewel"*, he says of his last days at school.

"He lost no opportunity", so writes Mother, *"of visiting Winchester after he left, over and over again, and he and Winny* [Gilbert's second sister.] *and I spent there his last Sunday in England in May 1915, with the charm and beauty of the place at their highest. In Chapel the hymn*

> *'Jesus, still lead on*
> *Till our rest is won'*

was sung. The last service before going to the front in the Chapel of so many loved associations could not fail to be very moving".

I think that the early experience of unpopularity had two effects. It was only latterly that he ceased altogether to be on the defensive. He was sensitive to criticism, and Hermione [*His cousin, third daughter of General Sir Neville and Lady Lyttelton.*] says that even later it was a surprise to him to find that people liked him. The other effect was the determination so characteristic of his later school-life to destroy the evil in his house which had so oppressed his early days. Into this determination he flung a certain chivalrous ardour, the creature of his own experience. He may have been for a time even over-preoccupied in this direction. Perhaps preoccupation was given its particular shape by the *'political'* mould of his thoughts. He loved devising a *'campaign'* and enjoyed the drama of personal alliance and collision.

And so at Winchester, in the later years he was always both in conversation and in his letters forecasting new policies and reckoning up the forces upon which he could rely for the government of his House. *"I have not made you realize"*, he writes as a prefect, *"how extraordinarily thrilling a job I have got here, or how difficult a one"*. The nascent politician speaks there, but also the boy.

"Adorned sensualism" was his comment on a book whose style I had praised. And this instinct was unfailing — in a way the more remarkable because from the beginning he had an eager and unabashed appreciation of comforts and luxuries. It was not till the last year of his life, I should suppose, that he tasted the virtue of spare and orderly living. But he had a wholesome recoil from certain kinds of evil not merely as wrong, but as things which poison the springs of youth and joy. Writing from Winchester he says: *"I don't know how I should get along without books, poetry, beautiful things, etc."*, and again he writes: *"What a lot such words (as the Pope's, etc., in the 'Ring and the Book') bring into one's life of beauty and help!"*

He goes on to insist that the lack of positive interests, and ignorance of the beauty of goodness are largely responsible for moral evil.

As a boy he was already by instinct a man of affairs, with the keenest relish for the management of a situation, and a desire to be in the current of things happening, which was altogether too strong for the habits of concentrated study work. "*It is all intensely thrilling and absorbing*", he writes of a term in which he is governing his house, training a Commoner XV, editing the *'Wykehamist'*, speaking in Debating Societies, steering the small boys through their early days, following with increasing rage the infamies of a hated Liberal Government, dreaming of his own future and plotting in advance what Mother used to call his *'holiday campaign'*. In all this he moved with a certain mature sagacity and with a precocious skill in the thrust and parry of argument. He seemed to combine a child's zest and impatience with the width of interest of a much older man.

As an athlete Gilbert never achieved much success, though Mr. Fort [*Second Master at Winchester.*] records a pleasant impression of him on the football field: "*he went forward [to the front] as he used to do in the old football days not like a born runner, if the truth is to be told, but so filled with the spirit of the fight, and with the idea of getting forward, that there was no room left for any fear, and no power on earth could have turned him back*".

As a small boy he showed a good promise at cricket, and had a style amusingly formed in the *'grand manner'*. He had the bad luck to miss a year's football owing to the effects of a serious but quite temporary heart illness, brought on from overstrain in walking at the Riffel-Alp, and though he was put in Commoner's Six that year with a view to his being 2nd Captain, he had to stand down the following year — a bitter disappointment which he met with admirable good temper.

Throughout his schooldays as indeed always Gilbert's loyalty to his home was unwavering. From it he instinctively derived his estimate of values — in it he was most unaffectedly happy.

He had none of the *mauvaise honte* of many boys when their *'people'* descend upon their school, and he was always pleading for one or other of his family to visit him.

I remember the almost embarrassing fashion in which he *'boomed'* one of his brothers who was to preach in chapel, an occasion which surely would justify an agony of apprehension in a school-boy. Indeed though I never heard him boast of his own considerable triumphs in debate and elsewhere he always greatly enjoyed any success achieved by any of us. Above all it was Mother with whom Gilbert shared unfailingly both his sorrows and ambitions. She was his constant audience, and he never lost the tender ways of a child with her.

He used to turn back to his home with eager delight in its distinctive atmosphere. And from beginning to end he was a centre of extraordinary interest and vitality. I also add these extracts from one or two Winchester friends.

From the Bishop of Southwark, Dr. Burge
(formerly Head Master of Winchester)

Aug. '15.
There are many many moments that Gilbert and I spent talking of deep and high things ... one seems to stand out amongst them all; the last Sunday of Cloister term '10

OXFORD

— *Gilbert's last at school. He and Macandrew* [Macandrew (New College) was killed on Wednesday 23rd December 1914.] *talked to me all that evening of their experience, as juniors and leaders, their difficulties, trials, and unexpected victories; and we planned how such victories might be made more certain for those who came after them. . . . He was so loyal and chivalrous, he lived his life out full of enthusiasm and high hopes and right ambition the glow of it all had never begun to fade one whit."*

From Mr. Beloe (formerly Master at Winchester)

**The Headmaster's,
Bradfield, Aug. '15.**

"... We at Winchester who loved Gilbert knew he would do something big some day, and now he has done it, and none of us dreamed it would be this. How I did love his ruddy head, his faults, his gifts and himself."

From the Rev. Guy Hanbury

Portsea, Aug. '15.

"I always had a great regard and admiration for Gilbert — and I know in our House at Winchester he had a real force for good. ... I know there are many others who, like myself, will never forget, and will be always thankful for his example at school."

In October 1910 Gilbert went up to Oxford, to Christ Church. He soon became a member of the Union, where he was successively elected Secretary, Treasurer, and President. As President he followed a good family tradition — his grandfather, father, and elder brother all preceding him. His deep interest in politics, his lively way of sharing in the life of the place in many various ways, would, I believe, in any case have hindered the keen interest in *'Greats'* (taken up directly after passing Pass *'Mods'*) which we all looked forward to for him; and also a very early and a very strong and as it proved — a hopeless attachment [*About this I should like to add what Gilbert wrote when it was all at an end: "... I shall never forget that I was the better man for several years because of you, and that you did me good only pure good and not harm".*] came between him and steady, concentrated reading. And though during this time the astonishing vitality of the boy, his high spirits and delight in all forms of life seemed (to outward appearance) unaffected at home and at Oxford by so strong and often so depressing an experience it must be said that continuous interest in philosophy, classical history, etc., fared badly, and no hard work in the later time at Oxford could overcome the drawback of its absence in the earlier years. Of his four radiantly happy full Oxford years he writes to his father (1 June 1914): *"I hope you will be able to feel to some extent, what I do — that I can't regret a minute of Oxford in a way. They have been four incomparable years, crammed with* interest and good fellowship, and I feel that in all the things I've learnt of all kinds, and in the mass of interesting people I've met, I have been amazingly blessed and lucky. And I wouldn't have missed my Presidency of the Union for ten Firsts."

Gilbert's second brother, Neville, whose time at Balliol as Fellow and Chaplain ran alongside of his own at Christ Church, as undergraduate, has written what follows about this part of his life.

From Neville Talbot, Fellow and Chaplain of Balliol, 1909-14

"At Oxford we came together of course very much, though I wish now that we had met more. We tried to keep to a weekly luncheon together. But both his life and mine were what may be called torrential. Certainly he was caught up at once into little less than a whirlpool of interests and experiences. They were by no means merely Oxford experiences. He was one of those modern undergraduates in whose orbit London bulked to an extent I imagine little known to earlier generations. His love affair, the House of Commons and theatres, and latterly Chelsea Hospital drew him often to London. At the same time he managed to drink deeply of Oxford itself. He made many friends, not only in Christ Church but at other colleges, and especially in Balliol. His social life was very full and marked by much conviviality — too much, so it seemed to me who as don and dean was grappling with undergraduate incapacity to say 'No' very irregular, and yet saved from its main inherent dangers by a native wholesomeness, a central loyalty to goodness (lit up for him by home association), a real though not fully operative basis of religion, and above all by a longing and determination to take his place on the right side in the conflict for the Kingdom of God.

He was very loyal to me and to what I cared for, and was a great stand-by at some times of crisis at Balliol. Though 'we say it that shouldn't', he delighted in his relations. On the other hand, with something of a don's limitation of vision, I think I overlooked the strength and colour of the moral impression which he made on fellow undergraduates. It was, I suppose, a tribute to his character that he was elected secretary and president of Junior Common Room at the House — offices usually held by prominent athletes. I recall the almost brazen way in which as president he summoned a crowded meeting of J.C.R. in order that I might explain about the Bishop of Oxford's Mission, which Ted was helping in and I was helping to organize."

Politics was the chief door by which he entered into Oxford life. I say the chief door, for there were others. He had time to become a genuine House man, and was particularly fitted to enter into the great diversity of that society. He had in particular one very warm ring of friends, of whom Roger Draper was one. They were simply fellow contemporaries at the same college, and had no touch with politics. A House man writes: *"All the time he was up he was a considerable person the life of the House"*. Still politics was the main focus of his life at Oxford. He made his chief friendships through the New Tory Club — which he helped to start, and as treasurer I imagine all but ruined — the Canning and the Union.

He soon became the chief figure at the Canning, and was secretary by the end of his first year. He made his mark at the Union as a freshman.

Through seeing public men, and in particular Arthur Balfour, at home, he brought to undergraduate discussions an unusual familiarity with the greater political world. Indeed, at the Union, he had to overcome a natural surprise in others at his mature parliamentary manner.

Undoubtedly his distinction as a speaker arose rather from his speaking and debating capacity than from what he had to say. Politically he was feeling his way. Three things only were clear to him:

1 Attachment to the Tory Party, and an even greater aversion to their opponents.
2 A passionate personal devotion to Mr. Balfour, [*"... I loved Gilbert he was always delightful to me, and I cherished the most confident hopes that if he lived he would do great things for his country. He has done great things the greatest and most enviable but not in the way I expected..." (From a letter of Mr. Balfour's.)*] of which instances are given below.
3 A great sympathy with ideals of social and democratic betterment, which he believed that the younger men of the Tory Party might make it their ambition to realize.

In my experience at the Union there were other wittier and more substantial speakers, but none so really endowed with the capacity for debate. He was much better at joining in a discussion than in opening one. He had by nature an advocate's gifts of reply and cross-examination. Yet he debated neither to score points or for cleverness' sake, but rather out of enthusiasm for his own case.

The occasion I associate most with his debating powers was a meeting of the Canning. He read a rather slight paper on Arthur Balfour and the Conservative Party. The paper was followed by a discussion which went heavily against him. Benison made an exceedingly lugubrious speech by way of supporting him, and this played into my hands as a Radical critic. One or two new members thought they would side with him best by airing the very crustiest Tory sentiments. Bobby Palmer made a smashing attack from close range, etc., etc., and I kept wondering how he would manage with his reply at the end of the discussion. But he arose quite untroubled, and with a very precise recollection of what everyone had said ran all the beads of the discussion on to the thread of supposing that *I* had carefully plotted beforehand the disastrous course of adverse or fatally-friendly speeches.

Arthur Balfour

He followed me *'on the paper'* at the Union in a debate on *'The Social Policy of the Liberal Government'*, but the chief remembrance of the occasion which I retain is the vivacious scorn with which he dealt with an interruption of mine.

As president of the Union he had the great fun of having Mr. Lloyd-George down as a visitor. It was at the height of that statesman's unpopularity. Both young Tory Oxford and some representatives of militant Suff-ragism hailed the occasion

David Lloyd George

as an opportunity for a demonstration. There was real risk that proceedings inside and outside the debating-hall might end in tumult and assault. But Gilbert bossed the detectives, and focussed the crowd and controlled the House with great masterfulness. The manner and success wherewith he crushed a member, who, in asking an insulting question about Marconis, had keyed the whole House up to taut expectancy of a row, is unforgettable. Rising very promptly from the chair, with inimitable *gravitas* he said: *"I feel sure that I am only expressing the unanimous opinion of this House, of whom the right honourable gentleman is the guest, when I say that we will not tolerate any insulting ..."* (the rest drowned in roars of cheering). It was as he prophesied of it, *"the evening of his life"*.

We can leave speculations as to what his Oxford promise would have brought him to. The single and simple summons of war and the exactions of training came, I think, to him with a certain peace after the turbulence of Oxford and its many delights and experiments.

His hands were full as he offered himself, and part of the fullness was thankfulness for Oxford.

He has passed on, crowning the stages of his eager growth with achievement. It is terribly dull for us that he is gone.

The extracts from letters which follow are those to which reference is made above, as illustrating his admiration of Mr. Balfour:

I. After a visit of Mr. Balfour to Farnham

April 2nd. '12

"... The week-end has been intensely interesting. A.J.B. can never have been in better form. ... As usual, I was quite overpowered by the charm of the man. It's simply the size of the intellect which first strikes one — in a different class to everybody else's in the room. Then it's a perfectly regulated, beautifully luminous mind, that has no difficulty in giving its thought expression in perfect sequence, without any effort or straining after effect, but with the most absolute grace and charm. At times, when one listens to him talking, one suddenly seems for a second to see what he is seeing and to rise to a wholly different sphere of thought and imagination. And then one loses it, and one feels that he is soaring in regions where one can never follow him. At luncheon on Sunday, when I was sitting next to him, he talked to me eagerly about some new books that had just been written in connection with my work at Oxford. By the mercy of Heaven, I was on the whole tolerably well up in the points he dealt with!"

II. Account of an Open Meeting of the Farnham Field Club, when Gilbert opened the Debate on 'Is England Decadent?' and Mr. Balfour promised to speak.

26th April, 1913. Farnham.

"... *The place* [Farnham Corn Exchange] *was packed. Father was in the chair and gave the whole show a start with a few 'chairming' remarks. Then I arose! On the whole I felt pleased at holding their attention all through. I lost my nervousness after a little while, when I got interested in the subject and felt excited about it. It was a biggish hall and I found I had to shout rather. I wish my voice was more resonant. I tried to avoid making any positive statements, but rather tried to clear the ground of the subject, and suggested one or two possible theories to account for the extraordinary way nations rose and reached a climax and then declined — and asked whether this process could be avoided in the case of England. My chief object was to put some questions which I hoped A.J.B. would take up. Well, as I say, they seemed to listen to the argument, and Father and A.J.B. were both very jolly about it and seemed pleased. Two speeches followed, one from a young barrister called Livingstone, who had been president of the Union at Cambridge. He spoke shortly and very well, and made several points which interested A.J.B. Then Mr. Balfour wound up. It was a beautiful bit of argumentative speaking. I've never admired his mind more, or felt it more above any other that I've ever known. I was awfully pleased with the way he took up points in my speech and discussed them.*

Well, the whole thing ended most enthusiastically, and we came back to supper, and then A.J.B. sat up talking in the most fascinating and animated way till 12.30. I felt absolutely limp after it all. I've never felt a reaction more. I went to bed worn out. ..."

The strength and depth of his friendships at Oxford, the enthusiastic belief in his future and the good influence he had among those who knew him well, these letters will show and they are but a few which it was our great happiness to receive.

From Mr. Sidney Ball, Fellow of St. John's

The Union Society, Oxford, 4th August, 1915.

"... *I had the greatest admiration for your son's character and aims, and the greatest faith in his ability to make them good. Of all the younger men with whom I have been associated, he seemed to me to have the finest and the surest promise. In his sense and understanding of public duty and responsibility, he stood out as few men have done in his generation. ... His life would have meant much: one dare not think that his death has meant less. ..."*

From J. A. R. Marriott

Worcester Coll., Oxford.
"... As secretary of the Canning and in other ways, I came into very close touch with Gilbert, and conceived an immense admiration for him. There are few men in the Oxford of late years whose death will be more sincerely mourned by a wider circle."

From Rev. W. J. Carey

H.M.S. Warspite.
"... I needn't tell you anything about him you know far better his weaknesses and his strength. What I knew and loved him for was the idealism which underlay his mind and outlook: he was passionately keen on the ideals of a wholesome life."

From Spencer Leeson

Aug. '15.
"... All his Oxford friends and they were very many were quite sure a brilliant career in politics lay before him. We used to think his powers grew immensely from year to year, especially those who heard him each week at the Canning Club, which I think possessed a larger place in his heart than anything else in Oxford of the kind. We frequently spoke on opposite sides to each other there, and I have learnt a very great deal from him. But a brilliant life has been nobly ended. His energy and force will always be an inspiration to those who knew him, he had a great gift for stimulating other people, and once or twice he gave me most valued help and encouragement. ..."

From A. P. Herbert

Royal Naval Hospital, Plymouth.
19th August 1915.
"... I saw a good deal of Gilbert our last three years at Winchester, and a great deal at Oxford, and more and more loved and admired him the better I knew him. ... He was a most inspiring person to do things with, and we all expected the greatest things of him. ... Later on, you may like to remember the very deep and sincere admiration and regret of a humble companion of his youth. ..."
[A P Herbert attended Winchester from 1904-1909. During the war he served with the Hawke Battalion, Royal Naval Division.]

OXFORD

From Eric Benison
(who died a few days after writing this letter)

Breakwater Fort, Weymouth.
9th August 1915.

"One of the very last times we met was on a Sunday morning in the winter, when we went together to St. Paul's. What caused it I know not, but the thought stole irresistibly over my mind that we should never be there together again. Day after day as I read the casualty lists it was his name that I feared to find, for of all the men I have ever known and loved it was Gilbert whom I could most ill afford to lose. The walks that we walked together in the happy ways of Oxford — the dinners that we held, and the speeches that we made, and not least of all those when I was his vice-secretary in the Canning — return and will return upon my mind. But more even still shall I cherish the memory of those hours we spent in the perfect atmosphere of his room, sometimes reading and talking and sometimes in silence; and, above all, of those when we listened as we loved to — to the music of those wonderful choirs. If ever a man influenced another for good, then Gilbert influenced me, and now it only remains for me still more even than before to try His works to do. Truly it was said of Mr. Alfred Lyttelton, but not more truly than of my own beloved Gilbert:

'This was the happy warrior this was he,
Whom every man in arms could wish to be'."

From E. F. W. Besley

British Expeditionary Force,
Aug. 15.

"... I wonder if you know how horribly I feel Gilbert's death: how we loved him in Long Wall, and what a tremendous elevating influence for the good he had on me in particular. That last will never be effaced. It seems so cruel, after all we talked and planned about his future, and discussed his thoughts all that last great year. ... For myself, Gilbert's loss as a friend and as an example can never be repaired. He had the gift of leading men, and he — perhaps unconsciously — was leading and, thank God, influencing me. I cannot flinch from a death now that he met so bravely. ... For me something very big is gone: there can never be another Gilbert."

From Walter Monckton

Aug. '15

"... Gilbert had the most vigorous, fresh and noble mind of any man I ever knew, and I know that his life has been and will be an abiding influence for good on those of others. ... He was the embodiment of youth and life and hope, and his great sacrifice of himself places all three on a higher plane. ...

P.S. 13th August.
I have been thinking so much of Gilbert these last few days, that I will add just a little to my letter before I send it. I have been feeling lost in the knowledge that I can't turn to him for help and advice, for all my plans and hopes and ideas were bound up with his, and I realize his strength of character and personality more than ever now also how very near the surface his faults were, and how deep and steady the goodness in him. ... He was the very best of friends, and as our intimacy increased so did my joy and pride in it. ... He will still be my greatest friend, and I shall often feel the kind critic's hand on my shoulder. And unless all our life is a lie, I know we shall all see him again. ..."

The problem of his profession was often a real worry to Gilbert, even in the middle of his Winchester time. He writes, 7 February 1909, from Winchester: *"I am worried as to my profession. I want to make up my mind. My dearest ambition is to get into Parliament, and my chief interest is, frankly, politics. But I know that this is impossible for a long time, and there is an immense lot to be said for the Bar. I like it, and think it is a profession, where as far as I can see I am more or less likely to get on. But then I wonder if it is a good plan to make it a stepping stone, and whether it is possible to do the best in a line in which one's ambitions do not really lie. I should so like to hear what you think."*

And again after speaking of various social problems he goes on (January 1912): *"... I want to lose myself in all these problems and interests. I would give anything to be able to do something which would be an infinitesimal share in the restoring of order and balance to English society. I want to lend a hand in the fight against poverty and misery and wrong. It is this that draws me into politics. The desire to be constructive, to create, is overwhelming. My greatest ambition is to be among the great world problems and to try and give my part to their solution — to forget myself and my own interests."*

I think as the years went on he had hopes of being able to get into business, in a way which involved looking after employees, and that this might have been compatible with getting into Parliament while still young.

Both he and Oliver Lyttelton had always contemplated going to the Bar, and Gilbert was eating his dinners during his time at Oxford. He greatly enjoyed acting as Marshal to Sir Walter Phillimore and to Sir Charles Darling, and entered keenly into various criminal cases, often going into Court.

I think the definite, and, until the War was over, the unquestioned rightness of his serving in the army produced a feeling of quiet and satisfaction which made his soldier's life very happy, though his ultimate choice of a profession was but *postponed*. The combination of having to earn his own way in the world, and the intense desire to serve his country in the House of Commons and in working with kindred spirits for the betterment of England, was never long absent from his mind.

Gilbert's great love of his home has been mentioned more than once. One feature of this was his delight in long talks with his father for whom he had an extreme veneration — lasting, it must be said, into uncouth hours of the morning.

Home

His visits to his sister May at Repton and Harrow were, too, great pleasures to him. Her small boys he thought *'adorable'*, and he had endless fun with them at Harrow and Farnham. May writes: *"I delighted in his visits here. He used to arrive (preceded often by a telephone message) full to the hilt of plans and wishes, and more than prepared to make of 'The Headmaster's' that pied-a-terre for London which we accused him of making it. We used*

Repton and Harrow

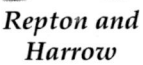

to chaff him about this, as the latchkey was pressed into his hand, and we knew that he would arrive home in the early hours after the Play, and go off to London next morning after a late breakfast!

He always arrived brimful of affection and chaff — a real interest in one's life — and he was very appreciative of the like in return.

I have a vivid recollection of the dinner I had with him and two friends, in the garden of 8, Long Wall Street, on the last Saturday evening of his last Summer Term at Oxford. He was so eagerly pleased at the dinner — which was 'just so' — being laid out in that fascinating little garden; he was so eagerly happy at being host so good a master of the ceremonies. He did not let me go without getting some music out of me, and so rounding off the evening — to fill the situation out to its limit was what he was out for always."

For Lionel Ford he had the greatest admiration for his work as Headmaster, entering with quick intuition into his problems and methods. Lionel writes of him: *"... His conversational powers were extraordinarily brilliant. No one could describe a scene more picturesquely — not a point omitted or forgotten, not a touch of the humorous side of things missed. He loved to state a case step by step, almost as a leading counsel might develop his brief in an action at law, and I used to wonder at the mental processes by which he reached such easy mastery of the facts and such lucid marshalling of them in impromptu speech. He was quick to counter interruptions with telling repartee; would flare up suddenly if contradicted too flatly, but never failed to appreciate friendly chaff.*

We saw glimpses of him at Harrow during the year of his service training. He never pretended that he liked soldiering, or that he did not long for the war to end before his time came to be called to the front. But when it was clear he must go, there was no sort of repining or turning back, though he realized quite plainly the whole of the risk involved, and occasionally talked about it quite without reserve. I think what he dreaded was not death so much as a mutilated life; that would have been very hard for him to face, with his full-blooded activity and his intense joie-de-vivre. I sometimes said to him that I thought his life's motto had always been 'Let me taste the whole of it', and he did not disagree. [It was this which gave such high significance to his repugnance to the moral licence which the phrase is sometimes used to justify.] He has tasted the whole now, and not flinched from the last measure of devotion, which I am sure he had faced out in advance. I remember well one evening in my study at Harrow, when the conversation had drifted rather near the thought of that possibility, how suddenly he started out of his armchair and for a minute or two paced the room in silence, with a look in his face that the deep waters 'had gone over his soul'. We spoke no more till the tide was past, and then only on trivialities, but I never felt quite so near to him in tenderness and sympathy as in those moments, when I knew he was facing his Gethsemane, and I just dumbly writing by his side."

From Lady Gwendolen Cecil

The Lodge House, Hatfield.
"... I am thinking of the dear boy during the time (autumn of '11) that he spent here while you were in America — especially a long talk walking up and down in the garden, while he spoke of his ideals of manly purity and knightliness — so fierce in his scorn of the low standards that he had met with so anxious to assert the higher and do battle for the right: so ardent, so uncompromising, so confident: so young — and so superior in his youth to one's own cold, middle-aged acquiescence in what was. ... He sought for some high service and he has been called to the highest. ..."

I have found in Gilbert's letters several times a sort of questioning with himself on the great subject of self-sacrifice, and the offering of even life for one greatly loved. I think the following extracts have a peculiar significance in the light of what was to come.

To a Friend

Farnham. July 12th, '12.
"I spent last Sunday here, alone with Mother and a very attractive cousin, Bertram Talbot, whom I'm fonder of, I think, than any of my relations.
... I've always wondered whether I could give up my life for somebody else's. I suppose if one really acted ideally one ought always to let others be saved before oneself. Whether one would do it or not is another matter, as on the 'Titanic'. But I don't think that is the real test. The real test would be in some sudden moment of danger or crisis when there was no time to think, and what one did would be by instinct only. I mean if one saw a blow about to fall on someone which would kill them, whether one would save them by putting one's own body in the way. At such a moment I think only real love would make one do it — the instinct of perfect love in which one's own individual self is completely eclipsed by the person loved. I can easily imagine the situation in which it would be no effort to me to throw away my own life. I've always felt that Browning touched an extraordinarily true note when he makes Pompilia say in 'The Ring and the Book', as she lies dying:
O lover of my life, O soldier saint,
Who put his breast between the spears and me.
She couldn't pay a higher tribute to the depth and purity of his love. All this idea has always seemed to me the very quintessence of romance. It's this that provides the intense romance in the life of Christ, and in a lesser degree makes a 'A Tale of Two Cities' such a

great book. There seems to me to have never been said anything more poignantly human than 'Greater love hath no man than this," etc.

Of Gilbert's inner life, and the religion which stood him in good stead, I should like to say a little. As a child and boy he was delightful to teach from the Bible. His great love of beauty from early childhood made him delight in the services at St. John the Divine, Kennington. He often went there on Sunday mornings with his sister May, and he was very fond of Canon Brooke and of his sister, who kindly let him pretty often study the pictures of Tissot's New Testament, to his extreme delight. After the break at Southwark Cathedral he lost his early delight in Church services, except at St. Paul's and Winchester Chapel, but he always remained a frequent communicant, holding almost passionately the conviction that the realization of the Person of Our Lord is the rock on which Christianity rests and that union with His self-dedication was the spring alike of worship and of duty. This conviction was to go with him to his death, and there be sealed.
This it was which most powerfully affected him when he saw the Passion Play at Ammergau in 1910, and also which drew him so closely into the Mission at Oxford under Bishop Gore in 1914.

The Bishop writes (4th August 1915) from Cuddesdon: *"... I am so thankful that I was allowed to see something of his resolute religion at the time of the Mission."*

He delighted in fine and honest preaching, in particular I remember his appreciation of Father Stanton, and always of his father. His was, if it is possible to say so, a simple faith, curiously untouched in the deepest part by his Oxford reading, and by the ferments of modern thought. He was moreover a great reader of very modern books.

And it was all deepened by all that the last ten months of his life brought him, of experience and responsibility, and the shadow of danger and death over him and his friends. Six weeks before he fell he wrote from the front to a friend:

British Expeditionary Force.
June '15.

"I want you to have religion as a real thing in life. Sometimes I think you don't get the chance of knowing what it is. Try hard to get it into your life as the background of everything, and the great resort in trouble. It is not just a matter of being good, and going to church — it is romance — love — adventure — peace — beauty. Pray hard sometimes and pray for me when you do."

And, again, to Hermione Lyttelton:

British Expeditionary Force.
June '15.

"I felt comforted the other day out here when Neville came to see me. I was saying that one felt such an atom out here, and if one was killed, one would only be like a bit of

The War

sand on the sea-shore. Neville said the thing to think of was the penitent thief saying to Our Lord on the Cross, 'Lord, remember me', and then the infinite graciousness of the answer. The greatest drama of the world was going on, yet Jesus had the time to think of an obscure criminal."

In December 1911 he writes to the same: "*I am delighted that you were impressed with —. He is a really great man, and the services at his church are what I like. The religion there is not formal — it is alive — it is personal. I think there is in the minds of so many people a misunderstanding of what the Christian religion really is. It is not a philosophy, or a system of ethics; it is not a somewhat wiser way of talking about God. It is a direct revelation from God in the person of Jesus Christ. It all turns on what men think Christ to be. Christ was not the perfect man. He was God. The teaching of the Gospel is that God took man's nature upon Him, and as God dwelt among men that because He became a man, and because He was God, He has given Himself as a permanent means of approaching God. That is the doctrine taught when Christ says, 'Come unto Me all ye that are weary … and I will refresh you'".*

Before leaving Oxford in June 1914, a most delightful offer had come from a great friend of Gilbert's, Geoffrey Colman, that Gilbert should be his travelling companion on a nine months 'trip round the world, starting, in July, with Canada, and including visits to Japan, China, and India. No proposal ever received so delighted, enthusiastic, and grateful a welcome, and the plans and arrangements and joyous anticipation and novelty of the great trip made the months full of joy.

Harlech. Easter Day 1914.
"… *Meanwhile, my chief and all-important item of news is in Mrs. Colman's letter which I enclose — with the most magnificent offer for me to travel with Geoffrey round the world, and paying for my fares. … I've been delirious with joy since it arrived. … I've not to go as tutor to anyone, but simply travel with a most delightful friend and companion. It's like a sort of miraculous gift in the Arabian Nights. Since the letter came I've done nothing but hug myself with excitement in the intervals of work. Just think of the luck of it! I do feel so horribly undeservedly lucky at this wonderful chance falling into my lap like this. I've written a long letter to Mrs. Colman in which I've tried to tell her how grateful I feel. … I do feel so awfully grateful and thankful. I think an offer like this falls to the lot of very few people. … And I am trying to be thankful before GOD. …*"

The War

But just before they started on 31 July 1914, there had come the shadow of the War, and though, hoping against hope, they did get off and got as far as Quebec, Mrs. Colman and I felt — and our sons felt — on the platform of Liverpool Street Station, that probably England would be involved, and that both would have to return to take their part in the War. And so it was. Even on the voyage out, a German cruiser pursued their ship — the *Calgarian* — the whole way across the Atlantic, without the passengers knowing of it — though they were requested to close all the port-holes at night — the ship rushing through the night without any lights. It was only on arriving at Remowski on the St. Lawrence River, where the ship was received by a crowd of people with band and Union Jack flying and *'God save the King'*, that any of the passengers knew that war had been declared, and of the grave danger they had been in or realized the admirable coolness and pluck of the captain. Wireless telegraphy had informed the Canadians of what had happened. After a most depressing twelve hours in Quebec, the keenly-disappointed friends returned in the next ship to England, where they at once sent in their names to the War Office, and in September found themselves in an officers' training camp at Churm, alongside countless university and public school men.

A month's most strenuous training was got through in beautiful weather, with a considerable amount of enjoyment and zest, in most congenial company. Gilbert shared a tent with Mr. Kay-Shuttleworth, and they were devoted to their Colonel, Colonel Maclachlan, afterwards Colonel of the 8th Battalion of the Rifle Brigade. The friends were given commissions in the 7th Battalion of the Rifle Brigade.

It was the deep and earnest conviction in the righteousness of the cause for which England joined the War, that made Gilbert a keen soldier, and this conviction grew and deepened as the months went by. He did not wish any more than before the outbreak of the War to take up soldiering as a profession, but he did become a most keen, efficient and strict officer, delighting in the learning of so much that was new and interesting, and especially in the responsibility of having the fifty-four men of his platoon under his direct control, and watching their development and excellent progress. The bottom of it all and of the kindling enthusiasm was the great cause of freedom for which the Allies were fighting.

He writes from Churm to Hermione Lyttelton:

Churm.
September 3rd, 1914.

"… This isn't play. We drill and are lectured to for ten hours a day — the most utterly tiring thing I've ever done. But I'm taking to it rather kindly, and when one reads the papers it's good to feel one's doing every bit one can …"

… Whatever else is true of life, one thing is certain that I am doing the right thing now and that every ounce in me must go to it till the end. The War is amazingly inspiring, and all the Belgian stories and all the devilish and damnable horrors that these swine inflict on the women and children make one long to get there though I don't flatter myself

The War

I should find war congenial! ... It's all magnificent really it's purging us all. ...

... I can't imagine wanting to be a peace soldier, but it's wonderful to be doing it now. And I still can't help reading the war news and the casualty lists without a sense of wondering whether some day one's turn will come, and whether it is possible to imagine a finer thing happening to me, and which at the same time would deal for ever with all troubles and difficulties in this world. ..."

After the training at Churm, his Brigade was quartered at Aldershot and Bordon and back again to Aldershot; he constantly came over to Farnham and also brought over his friends. He delighted in the very warm friendship that he made with his fellow officers. A life so concentrated and in such close quarters, with all the immense reality understood in a kind of quiet and silent way between them as to what it all meant, made a few months' friendship greater and deeper than many of a much longer time; they shared too in a very great and genuine pride for their Brigade and Battalions.

The following extracts from officers of his Battalion and others, written after the fatal day at Hooge, show what this friendship was.

From Col. Heriot-Maitland (O.C., 7th Batt. Rifle Brigade)

Aug. 1st, '15.

"... Gilbert's strong character and his devotion to his men and to his duty were beautiful. It is some satisfaction to know that he was attacking the enemy at the time, and that it was not the result of a stray bullet in the trenches."

From Sir Archibald Hunter (G.O.C., Aldershot Command)

Government House, Farnborough.
4th August, 1915.

"... Your son was loved and trusted in his Battalion and was an honour to it."

From Major H. D. Ross (2nd in Command, 7th Batt. Rifle Brigade)

5th August, 1915.

"... Gilbert died leading his men. No one could have done more. All the men of his company were very much attached to him, and when we heard in the middle of the action that he had been hit, several men at once volunteered to go and bring him in, although the enemy's fire was still very heavy. Two lots started, but as the men in each were hit, the attempt had to be given up. To us he is a great loss, as he was always in good spirits and cheery, and had something amusing to say."

The War

From Capt. E. J. Kay-Shuttleworth, 7th Batt. Rifle Brigade

3rd August, 1915.
"... I should like to tell you how last I saw him rushing gallantly forward to the attack: he was about 50 yards to my left and was passing just behind a little knoll, waving his arm and calling to his splendid men to follow him, which they did, in a magnificent attempt to regain what had been lost in the early morning through liquid fire.

His humour, his great fund of good stories, his wide reading and many interests all made him a wonderfully good companion out here.

As you know, we shared a tent last September at Churm, we shared a room at Aldershot later, and we have always been together out here. ...

I cannot express to you how much I miss him. ..."

Sergeant J, L. Chumley (now a Commissioned Officer)

Aug. '15.
"... Lieutenant Gilbert Talbot was a brave, fearless leader, strict on parade and yet highly respected by all ranks. He and I were the best of friends, and no man in our Battalion will feel his loss more acutely than myself. Had he survived last Friday's assault, I feel sure he would have been proud of the Platoon he spent so much time and patience in training. On his whistle, they advanced through that wood in one straight line, just as if they might have been on an Aldershot drill ground, although under terrific shell, rifle, and machine-gun fire. I am told his servant Nash behaved most bravely: although badly wounded himself, he tried his best to assist his master, and got hit a second time in his attempt. ..."

From L. Merriam, Lieut. 7th Batt. Rifle Brigade

Aug. 5th.
"I cannot tell you what a shock it was to see Gilbert's death in the paper. ... There is only one left from C Company. I was with Gilbert from the beginning of the war, and he always kept us so bright and cheerful, both out at the front and while we were training at home." [Gilbert and Mr. Merriam were billeted together for many weeks, near Farnham.]

From Mrs. Kay-Shuttleworth,
wife of Capt. Kay-Shuttleworth, 7th Batt. Rifle Brigade

Cambridge,
6th August, 1915.
"... Gilbert and Ted [her husband] had shared a tent at Churm and had already been friends before that, so that, before I was married, from hearing so much of him from Ted I felt I knew him quite well even without seeing him. Ted always said that Gilbert being

there made all the difference, and I could not fail to see that he realized what a lot they all owed to your son at the beginning, when things were most difficult. By his excellent example he inspired others to be keen. I do not think I ever met anyone more brilliant in conversation, and I shall never forget his talk and fun one wet day at Aldershot. ... Gilbert was inimitable, and I felt so grateful to him for his kindness to me. I know everyone loved him. He seemed to me rather special amongst all the others. I cannot rightly tell you how sad I feel that this calamity should have befallen our beautiful Brigade. ... I can only sit dazed at the misery of it all. ...

From Sergeant Shepherd
(one of the East Yorkshire Infantry men,
who brought in the body on 8th August)

"... We are only humble soldiers, but we all deeply sympathize with you in your great loss.
From the position of his body, which was in front of the other unfortunate men of the Rifle Brigade, who gave their lives in battle, clearly shows that he gave his life as a leader, and he must have been a very brave man to have got to the position in which he was. ..."

From Rifleman Dent

"... Having known your son over a year, I can honestly say that England has lost a man who would have made his mark in the years to come. ... He was loved by everybody, and we would all forsake an afternoon's sport when we were all in England to hear him at a lecture. When we were at Tilford he often lectured to Numbers 9 and 10 Platoons, and after one of these I remember a man of Number 10 saying 'I wish he was our officer: I could listen to him for hours'. The night Sergeant Dawson was killed, he nearly cried, and reproached himself for letting Sergeant Dawson go out on such a dangerous undertaking — but it was necessary: a dead German was on our parados, and the smell was upsetting the men, so you see the body had to be shifted. ..."

B/3439 Serjeant Richard Douglas Dawson
7th Battalion Rifle Brigade
Died on Saturday 24th July 1915, aged 36
Commemorated on Panel 46 of the Menin Gate

Richard was the son of Edward and Jane Dawson, of Hornsea and husband of Maud Helen Sutton (formerly Dawson), of Mere Cottage, Hornsea, Yorkshire.

From Rifleman Norton

"... I liked him so very much, and so did all the boys in the platoon. He always was a very good speaker, and I could sit and enjoy it for hours. I would have gone anywhere with him, he had such a very good head. ..."

Gilbert's facility of speech stood him in good stead with his men, and his lectures were keenly followed and well attended, the men often preferring to come to hear him even on a holiday. Other Companies occasionally joined in too. He lectured to them on all sorts of subjects — the history and the traditions of the Rifle Brigade, straight talks on moral questions, the splendid advance of the Russians in November and December 1914, their tactics, German methods and their strength and weakness, etc.

Then, though he was very strict, he knew his men intimately and helped them in troubles of their own, and when any were killed he wrote most fully and sympathetically, with careful descriptions of where they fell, etc., to the parents and wives and so on. He greatly helped the Chaplain of the Brigade in making it easy for him to get into touch with his platoon, and encouraging him to do this freely, as did several other officers in his Battalion.

He took to heart in a very real way his Colonel's words: *"Remember you are responsible for 54 lives; not 55 — your own doesn't count."*

Then there was the fun: the lightheartedness of young men together, and Gilbert's particular cheeriness and love of good and amusing stories and encouraging spirit when things were depressing. His capacity for seeing the humorous side of a situation now stood both him and his companions in good stead. One of his fellow officers, writing of some amusing incident which had occurred in the day's work of training in France, says: *"Talbot's account of it over a cup of cocoa in Captain Drummond's dug-out at 3 a.m. made us shake with laughter for nearly half an hour."*

He began the plan of reading aloud in their rest times, and we have heard from many sources what the fun was and the shouts of laughter from his reading aloud of 'Some Experiences of an Irish R.M.'.

'Philippa's First Fox-hunt' was a special success. Captain Hardy, one of his fellow officers (alas, killed at Hooge a few days before Gilbert) sent home for another volume. *"I never heard such reading aloud before"*, he said.

After a rather long and trying delay the whole party was delighted to set out on 19 May 1915, crossing with that wonderful rapidity of organization which put the whole Brigade on to the ship from the train, and *vice versa*, in seven minutes.

Of Gilbert's two months and a half in France and Flanders the following extracts from his diary, etc., will tell their own tale. The early part was one of considerable enjoyment, with beautiful weather, and the marching across so much of the country between Boulogne and Poperinghe was very pleasant. Gilbert evidently was developing quickly on the practical side, and was a very resourceful, efficient officer, constantly in demand in all kinds of difficulties in camp and otherwise, and bringing in a lot of fun and good cheer with his talk and good stories.

From Rifleman Nash (Gilbert's servant, who so faithfully served him to the end) I gained the following impression of his position in his platoon:

Diary From The Front

Nash gave a strong idea of the high opinion the men of his platoon had of Gilbert — they liked his lectures so much and thought him so clever ('*a very learned gentleman*') and a born leader, who would have been followed anywhere. He seemed to be constantly consulted by different people. He was very strict with his men, but they liked him the better for that, and they appreciated his high tone, and his expecting the best out of them.

He dwelt on his great care for his men — as to health, comfort, etc. — he always saw to all being as well arranged as was possible for them before he turned in himself, not leaving it to the sergeants till he felt satisfied all was right.

He noticed how much tidier he became out in France — instead of getting at what he wanted by pulling things out anyhow, and leaving letters about, the letters he had were carefully tied together and the things left in order.

He was always in excellent spirits, was the life of the party in the crater, and very cheery, and very cool-headed in the trenches under fire. Norbury and he were two of the coolest.

He became very proud of the platoon, about which Nash had no doubt that it was' the best in the battalion'. He was a constant topic of talk. They were sure he would be captain directly. He kept up their spirits that Friday (30 July) wonderfully, and was very calm and confident.

He had, however, his serious times, and talked constantly of home, and of his first hoped-for bit of leave, due about two or three weeks after the Hooge attack. *"Is there anything from Farnham, Harrow or London?"* he would ask. *"What a treat it will be to get back to the Castle and see them all."*

Below are some extracts from Gilbert's diary, which he kept regularly, and took pains with:

May 20th, '15.

"… The small French village in which we are billeted is about thirty or more miles due west of the place where there's a famous salient in the British line and ten miles due north of Sir J. French's headquarters. Everybody arrived v. done, and it took a little time to find all our billets, get the men in and settled, though all the organization was good, and it was not till a quarter to four that I found myself free to go to bed. I am lucky, being in the house of a miller, with a pleasant tiled bedroom with a capital bed with sheets! The men are in two barns, both quite near me — quite comfortable, with lots of straw, though one of them has chickens and pigs as very near neighbours: in fact last night a pig made an entry and woke my sergeant by stepping on his face. The French are extremely friendly, and light French beer, coffee and food flows freely, though money is short among the men. Of course billets like this,

Sir John French

well away from the firing line, are very different from those close up. Everything seems as usual here, except rather an absence of men. In fact war seems more remote here than it did in England, except for the persistent dull rumble to the north and east. It's a real rest and refreshment, more like a picnic than anything else. The country is lovely and the weather fine, the crops and wild flowers and all the countryside are lush and luxuriant, and my hostess makes divine omelettes. Everybody is seizing the opportunity to get their clothes washed. Officers eat in an 'estaminet' where 'Bones' ['Bones' represents Captain Spencer Heneage Drummond. He was killed on 30th July.] lives, and have so far done well in our own and Government food, and the admirable French beer.

... an estaminet

Whit Sunday, 23rd May, 1915.
"The feature of this and the following days has been the amazing glorious weather. Not a cloud day or night — full moon all the latter and blazing sun all the former, mercifully just saved by a pleasant breeze. The country doesn't get a bit dry because of the extraordinarily good canal irrigation. The result is most gorgeous: rich, green country, amazingly fertile, with delicious pasture, and crops far in advance of anything in England. ... Heaps of the work is done by women in sunbonnets, but even so one wonders how they'll get the crops in. I've seen no young men at all."

May 25th, 1915.
"We made another fairly early start from our last halting place, and set out on the hot day's march, which was to bring us actually to the firing line. This proved to be a short one, only some seven miles, and we halted at a tiny village some 3½ miles short of the firing line, where we went into 'close billets'. The weather was hotter, and after our long marching we were glad we had no more. ... This farm where I write is the grubbiest I've yet been in. The barn where the men sleep was indescribably foul — filthy straw, old clothes, stale food, odd bits of equipment, etc., etc., etc. — all old and filthy and verminous; besides which were picked up over 2,000 cartridges (unused) about the place. This all shows that the discipline of some of the Terrier Battalions who preceded us is in these ways bad. Most of the men had to bivouac out the first night, and pretty chilly they were, though some still prefer to sleep out in rather ingenious bivouacs made of waterproof sheets. In the end, we got the whole place decent and a credit to the R.B. — refuse buried, all the old mucky straw got out and burnt and new straw laid

Billets in a farm

down. The Colonel came round yesterday and seemed pleased; only ½ the Company is here under my command, with Shoveller, a fellow-subaltern (he came over to Farnham once or twice); the other 2 platoons are with 'Bones'."

May 26th.

"The night we arrived, the Battn. was paraded and addressed by Sir Charles Fergusson, who commanded the 2nd Corps to which we are attached. You remember he did so well at the beginning of the war and then came home. He dined at Farnham one night and was most thrilling. His speech was jolly, and gave us news. ... Sir Charles made an encouraging and rather inspiring speech, also telling us to be careful of the instructions we're given about the gas and also not to be careless of needless risks in the trenches. So early to bed."

Sir Charles Fergusson

Monday, 31st May.

We're off to the trenches in an hour. I don't think you need worry about this go, which I think will be relatively pretty quiet. I can't help feeling merely rather excited and curious. Anyhow, here goes.

We started for the trenches on a hot evening (May 27th) and had a march of some 3 miles, arriving in the dark. Everybody's nerves were a little on edge as we went, being entirely new to the business. We were accompanied by a nice officer of the Terriers, to whom we were to be attached, but who talked in a cool way of it all that was bred partly of genuine familiarity and partly of a desire to impress us. And it was both

... marching into the line

interesting and exciting to hear the rifle fire grow louder as we approached and to watch the lights of the flares that both sides send up all night. I must honestly say that before we started, and when we got there I felt surprisingly unfrightened, and much more curious than anything else. ... When the men were in the trenches I got off my pack and put it into a dug-out and sought out the subaltern to whose platoon mine was attached. I found him an absolute boy of 18, fresh from school, who'd been out some 3 weeks. His name was Peake. I liked him, and thought him awfully plucky. After all the men were at their posts, he asked me to come with him and visit his' listening post'. ... Of course, I said I should like to go, so we went along to the extreme left end of the trench and crawled out on our stomachs into the crater, formed by a howitzer shell some 10 to 15 yards out. The worst part was the stink — a stink that soon gets terribly familiar, and which in this case was caused by several unburied Frenchmen who were close by and who nobody could get at to bury. The Listening Post reported to us that they thought they had seen the figures of 2 Germans working on their parapet. Just after this, the enemy must have smelt a rat of some kind, either having caught sight of the tops of our heads or heard something. But a machine gun opposite and some rifle fire began to let drive; but as we were well down on our faces in the shell crater, the shots went over our heads. We waited till it subsided and then crawled back. I was interested by all this, and excited, though there was nothing in the least unusual in it. Listening Posts are always out and have to be frequently visited by the subalterns. Usually it's perfectly safe work. ...

It's marvellous when one hears the stories of what men have stuck to out here. They said that in the winter, when the mud in the trenches came up to men's thighs, a party which started to carry rations up the communication trench at 9.30 p.m. failed to reach the fire trenches till 6 a.m., and then with half the stuff lost on the way. ... The real break was the unexpected appearance of Neville to luncheon with me — fresh from England — passing through as his Battn. moved north.

... These infernal labour people must buck up with the shells. I saw a Battn. yesterday, 200 strong only, which had been in and out of the same trenches for over 6 months, and for the time being they are really beat, done. It's heartbreaking. And with the ammunition everybody's confident we could bang right through to-morrow. But I don't want you to think we're gloomy. We're not. We're very lively and in good spirits and intend to remain so. ...

I saw an unfortunate Territorial shot in the head and killed in exactly the same spot as our rifleman of the day before — obviously the same sniper. I hated it intensely, and the utter uselessness of that sort of casualty made one realize that modern warfare is a wicked thing. But I was glad for the future's sake that I didn't feel squeamish a bit."

June 7th.

"I forgot to say that I attended an Early Celebration which Green-Wilkinson held for us, which drew a lot of people. It was moving rather, as we were all serious out there in the lovely morning sunshine our service was in the wood, with the R.C. chaplain saying Mass in the next field."

June 9th.

"... In the evening I had orders to take 100 men and act as carrying party to the 8th R.B. ... As it happened, this turned out rather an eventful night. I left at 8.30 p.m. and got to the 8th R.B. Headquarters at 9 ... I reported myself to the Colonel, Ronnie Maclachlan, who I was under at Churn, who was delightful — though very short of sleep ... He said that the Communication trench was quite impassable, owing to the heavy rain which had come after the great heat of the last day or two, and that the carrying party of the evening before had lost some of the stores altogether in the mud. Accordingly we were to go 'over-land'. It was a little risky, but much quicker. My 100 men were divided into 4 parts, each part to carry for a separate Coy. and we started. I went with one party myself — got there and back in about an hour. The path was muddy and there were a good many bullets flying about, but we were none the worse and deposited the stores. The one trench I went into was odious, ankle deep in mud, and water sometimes knee-deep. I got back to Headquarters

... a service in the field

about 11, and found that 3 out of my 4 parties were back, but that one was not! I sent the 3 home and settled down to a long wait. I had no idea where they were or why they weren't back, and we didn't know where to look for them. I got on the Field Telephone to the various Coys., but with no result. And I walked up and down the path outside the Brewery with Joe Parker, the charming Adjutant of the 8th, till we both got very weary. At last, as day broke, at ¼ to 3, they turned up. It appears that what with the deep mud and the heavy stores the men in rear had got cut off, from being unable to keep up, and so got lost. They couldn't find their way in the maze of trenches, and could do nothing but wait till they were found by an officer, who put them straight. I marched them home and sunk into bed at 3.15. ..."

June 10th.

"... We found the trenches deep in mud, slush and water. In most places one had to drag one's feet one after another slowly out of the mud. The reason why they were so bad was that these trenches had been held by a really tired-out Brigade for some 4 months, reduced by casualties and unable to keep the trenches in proper repair. It gave one some dim idea of what men went through in the winter. Well, we struggled into our trenches, very beat and covered with mud from head to foot, and I took over from Billy Grenfell, who was the subaltern holding the trench before me. This was about 2 o'clock, and we 'stood to' at once."

June 11th.

"By daylight the trench was not as bad as you might have thought. We soon got them dryer, flinging out the mud and water and putting down dry earth. There were certainly some dangerous places in them, where one had to keep very low. I got an hour or two's sleep in a dug-out, which was very odorous, in the morning, and then the day passed as days in trenches do. ... A tragedy has happened: one of the very best and jolliest of my platoon was shot through the head on my listening post. It was pure chance — a stray bullet — and very bad luck, as they were concealed in a good place. I was sent for at once just along the trench, and we got him into the trench. The doctor was got in due course and said it was utterly hopeless,

... brewing up in the trenches

as he was shot through the brain. We kept him in the trench, and he lived some 10 hours, but was never conscious. It was an ordinary enough casualty, hundreds happen every day — but I was sorry for it, as he was a very favourite little fellow, infinitely cheery and conscientious, perfectly simple. I'd have counted on him anywhere. I think I felt in him for the first time by personal experience how fine a soldier's death is."

Diary From The Front

June 13th.

"We slept and rested and ate and washed all this day and the night, and attended a church parade held by Green-Wilkinson.

Then early the next morning — June 14th — at seven we moved again some 7 miles. I won't say where, as I think it's going to be of some significance. ... Everybody has had parcels from home (which we looked for and welcomed more than much fine gold). ... Last night it was felt the occasion was too good to lose, and Phillip Collins (who is our Mess President) and Ted Shuttleworth went to the neighbouring town to buy supplies. So it was a fine evening. We hung the tent, which is open on three sides, with wild roses from the hedges, and discovered that we'd got some eggs, cherries, strawberries, and three bottles of champagne! We made an awful noise, and somehow it felt quite like Oxford. ...

Lloyd George speaking in the House of Commons in June 1915

To-day, June 15, ... I have been reading the papers. Nobody will make me believe that labour comes very well out of this war. Lloyd-George is wonderful, isn't he? I think you should keep an eye on the reports from this front for a bit too — though I know absolutely nothing."

June 15th.

"I left off just before we left our bivouac in that pleasant field some way back from the firing line at Poperinghe. ... We got orders about 9 p.m. that evening to get ready to move at once. When the company had fallen in the Adjutant came riding across the field and told us — the officers — that we were to be in reserve for a big attack, the main attack to be further south. ... We were further told that, as in all attacks in this trench warfare, it would start with a heavy bombardment, to

Poperinghe ... a view from the fields

start in this case at 2.50 a.m. and finish at 4.15, the last quarter hour to be particularly intense. The infantry would then try and rush the trenches. We were in the Corps reserve and ready to move up at any minute. We told the men a lot of this, and it was interesting as well as inspiring to see how everybody's spirits rose at once, and we marched off in fine form, the men singing and laughing like children. We had about an hour or more's march over the rotten French roads, and then halted about midnight at some huts erected for troops. Here the men piled their arms and were told to be ready to move instantly. Otherwise they could sleep where they were. The night was very chilly and misty, so that I've known better nights. I put my overcoat over me and slept till just after 2, when I awoke very cold and got up to walk about to keep circulation going. A fair number of officers were doing the same. By 2.50 most people were awake and listening eagerly for

DIARY FROM THE FRONT

The German infantry advance on the British line

the bombardment. It started punctual to the second, but it was disappointing rather to listen to. ... One expected a roar of artillery, being only four miles from the guns, and got only some very persistent and continual explosions, which didn't seem very loud. Between 4 and 4.15 it increased a lot, and at 4.15 we were all trying to imagine what the scene of the infantry attack was being like and how far successful. It was now daylight, and as time went on and nothing particular happened, we most of us went to sleep again. I with others found a heap of empty sand-bags and slept in the sun till after 8.

In the afternoon, about 5, of June 17, I met Harry Altham (who, as you know, is Staff Captain to our Brigade). He asked me to go with him to see the ruins of the town and of the famous Cloth Hall and Cathedral, which had been visible all the time from our railway embankment about ½ a mile away. I naturally went.

I find it very hard to give you any account of this expedition which fairly describes it, or to avoid writing mere journalese. It was, to start with, intensely moving.

One visited the spot which since October has been held by British arms in spite of attacks more violent and persistent than had been dreamt of, and near to which so many thousands of our finest men fell and are now buried. Everybody almost connects the place with some separate individual. It's a quiet little provincial town, partly industrious, and partly just beautiful with its Cathedral and Cloth Hall. The trenches were drawn in a close circle round it, and perhaps never have efforts so great been made to effect anything than the German efforts to burst these few miles. One is partly moved therefore and partly amazed. I despair of telling you what the place looks like. It beggars description. The suburbs of the town are comparatively intact, though most houses there have been shelled. But the whole inside is simply a desolation. You cannot imagine it being rebuilt. We walked through the streets and found not one house which was not a mere mass of ruins or just a big heap of bricks. Of course there are fragments that remain, some with

Ypres

Ypres Town centre before the war ...

Lieutenant Colonel Patrick Butler recorded in his diary: "14.10.14. 4.45 p.m. On Place at Ypres. Wonderful Town Hall. Coats of arms on roof."

He describes the town: "*Ypres is (or, alas, was) a very beautiful and quaint old town, containing wonderful buildings. The Place d'Armes is in the centre of the town, and along great portion of this is the historic building variously known as the Halles, the Linen Hall, the Markets, the Cloth Hall, and the Town Hall. This building struck my fancy in a way impossible to describe. In its vast ground-level vaulted chamber hundred of horses were stabled, while above in the great frescoed galleries soldiers were billeted. It was of grey stone, with a loft belfry that was in the process of restoration, and to which the scaffolding still clung. The roof was of enormous extent, sloping down over the wall from a great height, and on it, gleaming in the sun, were four painted escutcheons of the ancient Counts of Flanders. Behind the Town Hall was the Cathedral of St. Martin, a noble edifice. The houses round the square were all old, and had gables and overhanging eaves, and sun-blistered shutters opening flat against their walls. I marvelled greatly that I had scarcely even heard of Ypres; it was so beautiful.*"

Lieutenant Henry Jones wrote home on Monday 23rd August 1915:
"*...A few days back I was in the city whose name practically sums up the character of British fighting — Ypres. Never have I seen such a picture of desolation. Not a house standing; only skeletons of buildings, shattered walls, and gaping window openings, from which all vestige of glass has long since disappeared. The Church and the Cloth Hall are simply piles of débris. To walk along the streets is like a kind of nightmare, even when the Boches are not indulging in a spell of hate against the place. Talk of Pompeii — why, this puts it quite among the 'also-rans'. What a pathetic spectacle to see a whole city in ruins! Stupefaction and sadness at the wholesale destruction is my impression of this melancholy ruin of an historic town.*"

... and after the bombardment.

DIARY FROM THE FRONT

odd familiar advertisements — I saw one of Singer's Sewing Machines. Odder than anything is to go into any of the ruined houses. They nearly all show signs of being abandoned in panic, without their owners waiting so much as to pick up anything: half eaten meals are on the tables: clothes lie in confusion on the floors. Most people take away tiny little bits of loot: I put a few little lace bobbins in my pocket. And then we came into the famous Place. The Cloth Hall, roofless and ruined, lies all the way down one side, and the Cathedral is just beyond it. The whole square is covered with loose stones and rubble. As everywhere else in the town, there's not a living soul to be seen, except passing British soldiers. We wandered through the Cloth Hall and saw the fragments of the famous frescoes, and oddly came upon two hearses — pushed inside there by some chance. I didn't go into the Cathedral till the next day. It's not quite as big as Southwark and must have been very lovely. Now it's got no roof and there are huge holes in the walls, and the aisles are heaped high with fallen masonry. I saw two shell holes which made one gape, one by the Cloth Hall, one at the East end of the Cathedral, the last the biggest, 16 yards across and 50 yards round: we measured it.

Nothing has brought the war home to me as has this town. Its people had no connection with the war, no interest in the war, and their lovely home has been gutted until it's unrecognizable. I wish everybody in England could see it. Harry and I remembered that the last expedition we made together was to Oxford. I tried to think of the peace and loveliness of Magdalen and Christchurch on that May evening and to contrast it with the blackened ruins we were now seeing. And we thought what Prussian Militarism would do for Oxford if it could.

... About 11.0 (Sunday, June 10th) we moved to another lot of huts about ¼ of a mile nearer Poperinghe. In these huts we stayed for 11 days, waiting our turn. We had perfect weather and life was fairly leisured and pleasant. We spent the first day in putting up an Officers' Mess for the Officers of two Companys — B and C — made of sandbags, with a waterproof waggon cover spread over some poles on the top. We then looted some tables and chairs from one of the neighbouring houses which had been shelled, and the place was quite snug. We had a lot of jolly times in it these days. We just all fitted in for meals and had some uproarious dinners.

... troops in camp

The day after we arrived we were told we might go and get baths at the 6th Division baths. We went, and found huge tubs with almost unlimited hot water. I got into one and lay curled in it like a kitten — the first hot bath since I had left England."

June 21st.

"I had managed to get a message to Neville, who I knew was just north, and after I had spent an abortive afternoon riding in search of him, the next day he rode over and had luncheon with us. He was well and fairly cheerful, and found a great many friends from

Diary From The Front

Oxford and elsewhere in my Brigade: Billy Grenfell, Henry Bowlby, Geoffrey Colman and so on. He was rather envious of us in meeting so many people from Oxford, and wished a little he was chaplain to our Brigade not that he's not fond enough of his own, he was so glad to see Billy Grenfell. I like Billy very much indeed, as does everybody. Some shells fell a little way off while Neville was there, and we pushed him into a dug-out till it was over. ..."

Of this visit (21st June) Neville writes:

"I found Gilbert in a double Company Mess rigged up under canvas stretched over a beam, and we had a very cheerful luncheon. They are having some of the sort of 'picnic' days, which occur in a campaign — all the happier because they are still undiminished by casualties. ... Everyone was looking very blooming and brown and hard — they are a magnificent set of fellows — just young England at its best, and one's heart rises in protest at the thought of the shears of death. Yet they would never — mostly — have done anything better than this. I saw Gilbert again on July 22nd he passed me on Scott Holland's 'Bundle of Memories', and he was full of excellent talk about Oliver's book, 'Ordeal by Battle'. Both before and after luncheon

... an officers mess

and dinner G. read aloud the 'Reminiscences of the Irish R.M.' ... So they go up tonight to the scene of the successful mine explosion, which is rather beastly I expect. ... There is nothing more to say ... deep down beneath the chaff and manifold secularity of their daily existence these fellows mostly are simply self-committed and God knows best."

Towards the end of our stay in these huts, Neville appeared again and said he'd run across Charles Fisher [*Student and tutor at Christ Church.*] and that he wanted Geoffrey Colman, Neville and me to dine with him that night. Charles managed to send a motor to fetch us and come in it himself. It was delicious to get into a motor again, and more delightful to see Charles. He was in excellent and most characteristic form though sick and weary of it all. He has been out here from the start, working hard with his ambulance, and I gathered from Neville doing awfully well. ... We had an excellent and pleasant dinner and much reminiscent conversation.

June 22nd.

"... I was woken in the trenches at about 7 by heavy shelling right on us. I listened to it for a bit from my dug-out: big, high explosive shells fired from our flank right on the trench a bit further up from where I was. One pitched some twenty yards away — I thought in my platoon, and I thought I'd better go and see after them. I went along the trench and found we'd been very unlucky. A shell had pitched clean in one of my bays,

DIARY FROM THE FRONT

killed one man — a very jolly little man — instantly — blown the poor chap to bits and wounded four others, two badly and two slightly. These included one of my sergeants — quite young a corporal and two riflemen. It also buried two other men, who were naturally shaken. I was much pleased with the steadiness of the men — no panic or crowding or anything. The difficulty was that we couldn't get the two badly hit men out of the trench till dark, as the trenches at present are too narrow for a stretcher. The two slightly wounded men could walk, and went back at once to the dressing station. The two others lay in the trench all day in great heat and tormented by flies, and I'm afraid they had a very bad time. My sergeant had a bad experience: we could only move him a very little way, and when the shelling began again — as it did soon — he was twice buried by the debris thrown up by shells. He stuck it wonderfully on the whole. The other fellow — a great big young rifleman, as strong as a lion — was very badly hit. ... He lay in shocking pain all day, but managed to smile back at me whenever I passed, and was most grateful for any little relief we could give him. I've had a good account of him. We got them both out under cover of dark and back to the Dressing Station, and then they're put into motor ambulances and so back. ..."

... rescuing the wounded

This was the first time I've been under heavy shell fire. It's no good pretending one doesn't hate it. It's beastly. One can tell from the sound just which shell is coming on your trench, and they come swishing through the air with a sudden sprint at the end that one learns to know and dread. It's very hard to take it steadily. One feels like a rat in a hole, with nowhere to go and nothing to do and above all no way of retaliating. It's pathetic to see how the men feel this. They'd all feel it easier if they could hit back. It's the feeling of helplessness that tries them. One spends one's time going up and down the line trying to keep them steady and cheerful. They are wonderfully good on the whole, and so tender with any pal that's hit. ..."

After a bit we decided that the German guns had got the range of our trench so exactly, and that we should lose so many men, that we'd better evacuate the part where the shells most often fell. Most luckily there was another half-dug trench about fifty yards behind. Into this we retired, half my platoon and half another. The new trench was very shallow and half-made in parts, but directly it was dark we got them on working like blazes, and when we finally left it it was a jolly good trench. I don't think the Germans ever discovered it. Anyhow it was never shelled, and the trench we had evacuated was shelled regularly every day — which was most satisfying. We took great precautions.

Diary From The Front

No fires were ever allowed in the new trench, and no work by day, and we lit fires in the old trench and tried in other ways to make it give the appearance of being still occupied. … The Battalion lost pretty heavily as a whole, and the losses of the entire Brigade were undeniably heavy for just holding the line. It's certainly a hot corner. However, we got a lot of fun out of it all, and lots of laughter at our joint meals. We worked very hard at night making the trenches good, when we could get out of them in the dark, and slept quite a lot by day. … The whole country has got very luxuriant and green now, which makes the scars of the trenches less conspicuous, and also makes war seem still more of a pollution. The guns were very persistent, both theirs and ours, all the time. The number of German shells that don't explode is refreshing. One thing that is a great relief after one has been heavily shelled, is if our guns begin to get to work with effect. Just after we'd been pounded a bit, our guns let drive with a heavyish bombardment for about a quarter of an hour, and it was really delicious to see the sandbags of the German trench fly and see the huge explosions of the big lyddite shells. I don't know whether it's bloodthirsty, but there's no mistaking the satisfaction.

… We had an interesting lecture, and I was interested at seeing Allenby, the Corps General, as well as Vic. Cooper, who commands the Division. I also had some talk with Rupert Fellowes, who was at Oxford with me. …

There's not much more to tell. I was pleased at the way my men worked. My trench was good and safe and clean when I left it. We had some jolly times. Bones is in excellent and improving form and runs the Company admirably. His dug-out was a pleasant centre for meals and for hot cocoa in the middle of the night. …"

General Allenby

July 8th.

We were finally relieved about 11 p.m. last Thursday and got out. … It was perfect to get boots off and get clean and to change one's filthy clothes and to see my dear valise again. We all had mails and parcels, and everybody was bursting with joy at being out of the trenches. … By a great mercy, though the Battalion has lost quite a lot of men, no officer has been touched, so we're the same jolly party once more, and we make almost as much noise at meals as at Farnham in the holidays. Last night I was made to read one of the old 'Irish R.M.' stories aloud, and it was a roaring success and is to be repeated. We hope to be out for at least a week, perhaps more. And yesterday I got another magnificent hot bath. I've seen Neville again, though we're not next door now, as his Brigade's in the trenches, but he managed to get over to luncheon the day we came out.

I've only one thing more to say. You people in England should realize that when it is said that lack of shells loses lives, what is meant is not so much that we haven't enough shells when we attack, but that until we've got enough shells we've got to go on holding the lines at the cost my Brigade has had to pay this week, without advancing at all or gaining anything at all. And that is what will break any Infantry's heart, because the strain seems long and demoralizing and profitless. So we must have shells. When we've got enough, we're all quite certain we can get through. …"

LAST LETTERS

This was the last Diary we received. Gilbert was writing the last up on the evening of the 29th of July the day before he was killed; this he put in his haversack, and it was rifled by the Germans, so it is believed, during the week he lay out in the field before he was buried. The haversack was found on the ground close by, cut off, and empty — his field-glasses, revolver, and compass were also taken. I add a few extracts from Gilbert's letters in the last weeks.

To Hermione Lyttelton

June '15.

"At times one's thoughts fly back to all the precious things in England, a thousand times more precious now. I think of Farnham, Winchester, Oxford in summer. What Winchester meads are like on a ½ holiday in June — or Magdalen cloisters on a May evening. And one thinks of all the family and the happy times we've had — the love that binds us all, and Mother and all she is to me, and I don't feel ashamed of wondering fairly often if I shall see them again, and if so when."

To his Mother

June 10th.

"... I want you so much to feel as I do (I know you do) how this war and the trouble of my being out here, and away from you has drawn us together perhaps as never before. So that I feel our love the great fact of my life to cling to — and I can almost feel you beside me — loving me. I want you to know just what is in my mind. ... The chief feeling for me now is the feeling of nearness. Somehow, I don't feel as if physical distance meant anything. Your love is near me through all these troubles and dangers. Yours is so much the harder task. My duty here is plain and simple, and there's so much to do it's hard to stop and think you have the uncertainty and waiting. ... I do long to live as I write, but I'm in God's Hands, and I trust in His mercy."

To the same

July 22nd, 1915.

"... I feel so near you really. It's easier for me than for you. Death is not so formidable or awful in a way here. Soldiers put it in its right place somehow. I know it's not the end — only an incident — and that the love that unites us lives through and will triumph over all. But I do long for home sometimes."

Gilbert's last letter to Neville, giving a short account of the holding of the crater

July 28th, 1915.

Dear Bumps, [Neville and Gilbert called each other 'Bumps'.] — We've had the hell of a time, but the Company has been taken out of the fire trenches into a quiet support *point, and we go out of the trenches altogether to-morrow. I'm all right, but it's certainly the deuce of a place. French's communique about Hooge was really concerned only with my platoon and my trench! — which is amusing.* [Captain Drummond writes, 28th July: "We are very much pleased, at least my company is, and especially one platoon Talbot's, who did it. We have got a mention in the communique. The *'Daily Telegraph'* even gives it a big heading (26 July 1915), *'Bombs and Mines'* — near the crater."] *But it's all ridiculously exaggerated and overstated, and makes me think very poorly of communique's. And it's just an ordinary lie that the trench mortar is silenced. The guns never hit it, and it's been firing this morning. It's a sort of aerial-torpedo thing, bigger I believe than the ordinary mortar. It fires an enormous long shell, which goes a very great height and spins like a Rugger ball, and then falls with an ear-splitting and most demoralizing noise. It's very trying, and we've had a lot of nervous breakdowns. Ronnie Hardy was killed by it.* [Of Captain Hardy he writes in another letter: "Ronnie Hardy was a really perfect fellow. One of his platoon wrote home about him and said — 'Absolutely my ideal of an officer and a gentleman. God loved him too well to leave him long with us'."] *One fell on my trench. Thomas Gent was also killed on a bombing party. Shoveller and Merriam wounded. Also my dear Sergeant Dawson killed. But I'm all right. Laus Deo. Also a part of my trench was blown up by a mine but we were lucky there. I'm writing about it in my diary, which you will see. Come and see me when you can. I'll tell you my precise movements.*

... German troops marching to the front

I have thought it best to give the account of what followed by an extract from Mr. John Buchan's *'History of the War'*, Vol. IX, p. 99, followed by the accounts by two eyewitnesses, Sergeant Chumley and Rifleman Nash, Gilbert's servant. These are all printed in the Appendix.

Of the part played in this tragic story by Gilbert and his own gallant comrades and platoon, and of the last moments I shall say no more, leaving it to be said (as I think ideally) by his and our life-long friend and helper Canon Scott Holland. The little Memoir reprinted by his leave from the *'Commonwealth'* of September 1915 will carry the reader again over much of the ground which I have tried to cover, and will close the story in the way I should most wish it to be closed.

GILBERT TALBOT
by Canon Scott Holland

[Of Canon Holland, Gilbert wrote to a friend in 1912: *"Didn't you like him? He's a wonderful man. An immense intellect, combined with extraordinary power and force as a preacher. And human and full of fun."*]

We had not thought of tragedy for Gilbert. Somehow that had never entered into the dream that we dreamed of him. There was a lightness, a freshness, a buoyancy about him that told always of life to come. He was so young: and so ready for the frolic of being alive: and so alert and brimming and radiant. He took things gaily as they came along: and was ready for them all. He enjoyed the daily business of living with most hearty relish: and was always in the thick of it: and revelled in its activities and humour: and could talk it all over for ever and ever: and was keen for any debate that was going: and rollicked in the free play of wits: and loved argument and chaff, and social intercourse of every shade and shape: and could never tire of the good fellowship of old and young alike. He was alive at every pore.

And then there was so much high promise. He had the special gifts that carry men to the front places. He was wonderfully ready and effective in all forms of expression, whether by speech or writing. He always told at once. While a boy at Winchester he wrote a letter to an evening London paper, which wore an air of such weight and dignity that it drew into the field the leading Liberal organizer, in the belief that he was dealing with somebody of quite special importance, to the immense amusement of Gilbert's friends. On leaving school he wrote an article for one of the Monthlies on Public School Life and Morality, which was not only extremely felicitious in style, but was singularly wise, and strong, and complete. He seemed so young in himself; but he wrote with a curious profundity on a matter of this kind. And the same note of paternal experience would often amuse the Union, as, in his boyish lightness of demeanour, he spoke as a father to his boys, out of the authority of one who had seen and known a larger world than they. The truth was that he loved getting to principles, and had great grips on moral standards, and a very keen psychological insight. He analysed motives admirably, and had a remarkably good judgement on practical perplexities. I once called him in to advise a father on a very perilous and complicated bit of school ethics, and I was immensely impressed with his combination of courage and wisdom. He was perfectly clear and strong in his judgement: yet gave consideration all round: and took his part with an authority and a force that could not be bettered. He had shown splendid moral courage at school, and had dedicated himself for several years, first by careful planning and then by the exercise of authority, as head of his house and prefect, to purging school life of its pollutions, and to relieving the smaller boys from fear of wrong. He was as clear and firm as a rock on all such matters: and had been singularly brave in giving his principles public and practical force. Whenever I was tempted to criticize his airy and careless looseness of manner, I used to recall this noble record of his in an arena so daunting and difficult as the big life of a great public school.

His capacity in writing was shown at its best, at the close of his Oxford career, by the sketch which he was invited to write for the *'Times'* of the Prince of Wales's career in the University. It was just right. It was very real and true: it had no humbug: it was perfectly happy in touch and tone.

But his fame, of course, had been won rather in speaking than writing. And, no doubt, here lay his special excellence. It brought him to the front in whatever company he found himself. He was really irrepressible. Whatever society or club he joined, he became at once its secretary or its chairman. He inevitably spoke for it. He could do it so easily, so quickly, with such felicity, with so much effect. He had the style, the equipment, the manner, to perfection. He already wore all the air of a leader of his party, and was in delightful command of himself and the situation. He was at his happiest in pure debate. He seized on the weaknesses of his adversary with really marvellous acuteness. He had his own points admirably ranged and handled. They were valid and clear, and precise. And he backed them with materials which he seemed always to have ready to hand. At his best, in all this debating business, he was really first rate. He made everything that he said tell for its full value.

He showed this power not only in his favourite field, the Union, but when, even in his Freshman's year, he ventured to counter Mr. Belloc, after some public lecture on Rome, I think: or, again, when he challenged the dry and clever Mr. Mc Cabe, who had delivered an attack on Christianity which the Christian defenders were showing themselves but poorly able to repel.

As a debater he would certainly have gone far in after life. And he had high political ambitions. He saw visions of a better social order. He hoped for great things. His ideal chief was Mr. Arthur Balfour, at whose feet he sat. He delighted in what may be called the Cecilian temper — its alert and free intellectuality, its dialectical acuteness, its logical penetration, and invincible courage. But he also cared deeply for the large human causes that drew all hearts together to work for the better day. And this is what gave for him such a large attraction to Mr. Lloyd George. Ever since the visit of the famous Welshman to Oxford for his address to the Union, while Gilbert was President, a most singular friendship was struck up between them. The older man would pour out his soul to the young fellow,

telling him of his hopes of a Social Policy in which all parties might unite, so that, in twenty years, they might change the face of England in town and country.
Gilbert found himself irresistibly fascinated by this personal charm. For a time he fell back on Mr. Hyde and Dr. Jekyll as a reconciling interpretation of the man whom he knew and the Limehouse orator: but, after a time, even this explanation went under. Only two days before his death he wrote to Mr. Lloyd George a delightful and intimate letter, telling him of the deep gratitude to him for his work on Munitions that was going up from the hearts of soldiers in the trenches who once had hardly been able to bear the sound of his name: and recalling again the visions of national welfare which he had opened out for him to follow. Mr. Lloyd George had only just read the letter, when he caught sight of Gilbert's name in the Roll of Honour.

For it was to be a deeper note, after all, that was to be struck. Our hopes, our anticipations, our dreams had been all of life — a life that held in it such promise, such opportunities. Right across this came suddenly at a stroke the higher call, the gallant response, the swift silence of death, on the field of honour, in the hour of glory. He had given himself to the new obligation with dramatic decisiveness. For he had just started with a friend, Geoffrey Colman, for his great world tour, every detail of which had been carefully arranged for months before. The war broke out while they were crossing the Atlantic. They knew it first by the cheering and the bands with which the arrival of their ship was met at Quebec. They spent but six hours on land, and took the next steamer straight away home. Both joined the Rifle Brigade, with which Gilbert was associated by his Uncle General Neville Lyttelton, and by his brother Neville, Fellow of Balliol.

He set himself to the unusual training and discipline, and proved to be an excellent officer. His innate gift of leadership showed itself at once. He especially won the confidence of his men by his open talk to them about all that he wanted them to do and know. On being asked, in his military examination, what would be his first act when placing his platoon in a post of danger, he said: *"I should call them all up and tell them what they were expected to do"*. This was exactly right, and singularly characteristic of the man. He gained greatly himself under the stress; he shed much of his careless disarray and casualness. He learned to concentrate. He lived no longer with *'loose sleeves'*. He deepened in character. He thought more of others. He steadily got his own soul ready for the risks that he quite surely saw before him.

After the endless months, as they seem, of preparation, the last act came swiftly on. His Battalion was among the first of the New Army to be sent up to the front firing line. His brother Neville, who had been acting chaplain to his old regiment, saw him before and after his first bout in the trenches, and was struck again with the quick way in which Gilbert occupied the ground among his mates. He always took the lead; it all buzzed round him; it was *'Gilbert'* here and *'Gilbert'* there, and *'Gilbert'* everywhere.

After his first bout was over, he and his lot were ordered to hold one of those

Canon Scott Holland's Memoir

awful craters which one of our mines had carved out in front of Hooge. They held it, and had just come out of it, when the murderous attack with liquid fire recaptured it. They were turned back at once, after two hours' sleep, half-way home, to re-march the eight miles already covered, and to be ready for the counter-attack on the captured trench. With nothing but that cup of tea, after the marching, they had to work their way by a communication trench through a wood that was being heavily shelled, and then rush an open one hundred and fifty yards.

Gilbert's platoon had to lead the attack. He deployed his men on the edge of the wood, and made them lie down in a low ditch, until the artillery preparation was over. At the sound of five whistles, they were to make the rush. The whistles blew. Gilbert rose at once and leaped forward, crying: *"Come along, lads, now's your time!"* But the platoon had lost heavily in the wood, and, what with this and the tumult, only sixteen men could be found to follow him He ran forward pointing the way with his arm, bidding his servant to keep close up with him. He was hit by a bullet in the neck. He fell: gave a smile to his servant,

... charging the German line

Nash, who tried to stem the gush of arterial blood; and rolled forward on his face. He was dead. Other bullets struck him, and one went through his heart. Nash was twice wounded himself, and was forced to leave him lying there.

When the officer of the next platoon, who had been told to follow and support Gilbert, emerged from the wood he could see no platoon to support. There was not a man left who was not hit. The attack had failed. There was never any hope of its succeeding, for the machine guns of the Germans were still in full play, with their fire unimpaired. The body had to lie there where it had fallen.

... Germans stoutly defend their position

Only, his brother could not endure to let it lie unhonoured or unblessed. After a day and a half of anxious searching for exact details, he got to the nearest trench by the *'murdered'* wood, which the shells had now smashed to pieces. There he found some shaken Somersets, who begged him to go no further. But he heard a voice within him bidding him risk it, and the call of the blood drove him on. Creeping out of the far end of the trench, as dusk fell, he crawled through the grass on hands and knees, in spite of shells and snipers, dropping flat on the ground as the flares shot up from the German trenches. And, at last, thirty yards away in the open, he felt that he was touching young Woodroffe's body, another subaltern, and knew that he was close on what he sought. Two yards further, he found it. He could stroke with

Canon Scott Holland's Memoir

Sidney Woodroffe

his hand the fair young head that he knew so well; he could feel for pocket-book and prayer-book, and the badge and the wrist watch. He could breathe a prayer of benediction, commending the poor dead thing that had meant so much, to Father, Son, and Holy Ghost: and then crawl back on his perilous way in the night, having done all that man could do for the brother whom he had loved so fondly: and enabled, now, to tell those at home that Gilbert was dead indeed, but that he had died the death that a soldier would love to die, leaving his body the nearest of all who fell, to the trench that he had been told to take. He crowned his life by this act of heroic decision. He leaped forward himself and made his sacrifice: and died, as he called others to follow where he led. He must have known perfectly well what was before him. He had said, before, that the officer who had to lead the first platoon on such a venture, had only one possible end to expect. In his own case the hope was forlorn: and he knew it. But he never flinched. He called, *"Come along, lads"*, and he died with a smile on his lips.

A week later, on the following Sunday, his brother Neville again went out with three brave Tykes from a Yorkshire regiment, who leaped over the parapet, as soon as he asked their help, with a stretcher on which, under peril not so urgent as before, they bore back the poor blurred remains, to be laid to rest in a quiet cemetery, under a wooden cross, which a kindly Engineer cut out for Neville, and wrote on it, of his own will, a word of Peace.

There the body lies. But he has gone into another life than we had chosen. And

... collecting the dead from the battlefield

we cannot murmur. In the letters that pour in from his most intimate friends, even those who loved him in his home are startled at the witness borne, not merely to the superficial gifts of which they were so proud, but to the depth and strength of character with which he impressed some of the very best men of his time. They all speak of the elevation of tone which he forced upon his company: and how he had become dearer each year to them by this deep influence on their inner lives. He had lived for his last year in lodgings, in most happy companionship with as good a set of men as could be found in Oxford, chiefly from Balliol. It was more especially with them that he grew to his ripe manhood. He was steadily coming through his faults. And this was no light business. For nature, in endowing him richly, had also made for him a character difficult to handle and to discipline. He could not be what he was, without being naturally self-conscious and self-interested. By necessity he came to the front in almost any company in which he found himself. He could not help being incessantly before the footlights. This was inevitable. But it had its dangers. And then, at Oxford, his many-sided activities had prohibited discipline and concentration: and he had never girded up his loins, or put himself to real proof under the austere sifting of the Schools.

But all this was behind him now. The last year had begun the work. The training for the Army bettered it. The seriousness of the issues before him, to which he had given himself, gave the finer touch. He was ready.

And, as we think of the perilous moral turmoil of that public political career to which we, in our blindness, were committing him — its dusty and doubtful by-roads, its egotisms, its personalities, its heat of controversy, we can believe that, by the swift gallantry of self-surrender, by the *'splendid action on the edge of life'*, by laying down his life with a call and a smile, he has, in one breathless and unsullied moment, over-topped our best desires for him, and, at a stroke, by the Grace of Christ, has *'triumphed over Death, and thee O Time!'*

"Fear not! Ye are of more value than many sparrows". So he had written in the Book of Prayer given him by his mother, which he carried with him. And, again, *"Yea! though I walk through the valley of the shadow of death, I will fear no evil"*. He understood. He was forearmed. Let his soul rest in Peace!

H.S.H.

APPENDIX

I. The Fighting at Hooge in the last days of July 1915.

From Buchan's *'History of the War'*, Vol. IX, p. 99. And the narrative by Sergeant Chumley and Rifleman Nash of what happened on 30 July.

II. Extracts which give some estimates of Gilbert by different friends.

III. A few characteristic contributions of his own.

"Well, I have quite a stock of shrapnel and liquid fire for the rear line of the Germans"

I. THE FIGHTING AT HOOGE IN THE LAST DAYS OF JULY 1915

The account of the movement of which the charge of Gilbert's platoon formed part is perhaps best given from independent sources. The events of July 30 are described in a few extracts from Mr. John Buchan's *'History of the War'*, Vol. IX, p. 99, chap. LXVII:—

The fighting at Hooge at the end of July and the beginning of August had no strategic significance. It was only an incident in the eternal struggle of small-losses and small gains to which the policy of holding the Ypres salient condemned us. But it is worthy of special notice, both because of the desperate nature of the conflict and because it was the first appearance in battle of one of the new divisions. ...

... The British dispositions in July, owing to the coming of the first detachments of the New Army, had undergone drastic changes. Here it is sufficient to note that on the 29th day of July the salient was held by the new Sixth Corps, under Major-General Keir. ... South of the Roulers Railway, in front of the Bellewaarde Lake and Hooge, and extending down to Sanctuary Wood, was the 14th Division of the New Army, under Major-General Couper. (It comprised the 41st, 42nd and 43rd Brigades, and was a light Division composed of light infantry.) ... Our trenches east of the Crater were occupied by two companies of the 8th Rifle Brigade from the 41st Brigade, troops who had just come up and had not been in these trenches before.

About 3 a.m. on the morning of Friday, 30th July, the Germans delivered a violent attack upon the trenches east of the Crater. ... The main attack that morning was not made by artillery. The enemy had sapped up very close to our line, and at three o'clock launched a torrent of liquid fire. The liquid was pumped from machines in the saps, and ignited itself in its passage. Now we knew the meaning of the accusation which had preceded the Crown Prince's movement in the Argonne. This liquid fire had been prepared since the beginning of the war, for we captured directions for its use in October; but the precise situation when it could be profitably used had not revealed itself until now. Combined with the fire was an assault by 'minenwerfers', those trench mortars fired from close range which our troops hated beyond every other weapon. The Germans, too, had a great number of bombers, who stormed our trenches with their grenades.

The combination of artillery bombardment, liquid fire, trench mortars, and bombs was irresistible. The two companies of the 8th Rifle Brigade were nearly blotted out. The Germans carried our first line, and won the Crater. Our troops fell back to the second line, which ran north-west from the corner of Zouave Wood. Thereupon the enemy began to plaster with shell the region behind our front, and turned the Zouave Wood into a death-trap. ...

The Fighting At Hooge

... The General commanding the Sixth Corps ordered a counter-attack for the afternoon of that day. It was entrusted to the 7th Rifle Brigade, which was brought up for the purpose from Vlamertinghe, seven miles off, and to what remained of the 8th Rifle Brigade. For three-quarters of an hour before it our artillery bombarded the German position, but without much effect. Far more deadly were the German shells, which swept Zouave and Sanctuary Woods and the country between and behind them.

The counter-attack began at 2.45 p.m., and was doomed to failure from the start. The battalions were mown down in Zouave Wood, and the few that emerged into the open fell under the blast of machine guns, They were under fire from the German fortins and from the German position on the Hooge ridge, and they had to face as well a devastating artillery storm. The Rifle Brigade never wavered, and no exploit in its long and splendid regimental history surpassed in desperate valour the advance of its new battalions towards certain destruction. Only a remnant remained in the trenches outside Zouave Wood. The fields and coppices were strewn with dead, platoons and companies disappeared, and few were the officers who returned. Among those who fell were two of the most brilliant of younger Oxford men, Lieutenant Gilbert Talbot of the 7th Battalion, and Second-Lieutenant the Hon. G. W. Grenfell of the 8th.

... The great counter-attack was fixed for Monday, 9th August. ... It was to the 16th and 18th Brigades that it was entrusted. The attack was made just before dawn. ... The artillery work which preceded it was admirably managed. ... Our infantry swept right up to the fringe of our own shell fire. Then the gunners lengthened their range, and our men were into the German trenches. ... The attack swept beyond the Crater, and carried the ruins of the stables. ... It had succeeded. Our losses were extraordinarily few. The two battalions who counter-attacked on the 30th July had had 2,000 casualties, including sixty officers. The difference in losses was the difference between a well considered and adequately-prepared movement and a hasty improvisation.

These clear accounts of the last few days' events are given by Sergeant Chumley, and Rifleman Nash:

From Ser*geant Chumley, C Coy, 7th Batt. Rifle Brigade* *(now a Commissioned Officer)*

24th August, 1915.

"... It would be about July 20th or 21st — rumour had it we were going into the trenches for twenty-one days.

We started off in the rain, but luckily we were conveyed to within four miles of the firing line by motor busses. On arrival at the trenches, we took up a position well to the right of the crater, but later found we were separated from the rest of our Company. During the night, D Company had manned the front of the crater, as well as the trench on the left, but owing to their losses from trench mortars it

Nash's Account

was decided they should be moved and so leave the crater unoccupied. At 8.30 the next morning, we received orders to occupy the left of the crater, previously held by D Coy, and by this means link up with the remainder of C Coy. During the next few days we were bombarded by trench mortars and had many casualties. One evening the Germans made an attack on our Platoon with bombs; we opened rapid fire and soon repulsed them. At the end of about four days it was decided we ought to be relieved things were so hot. I should have mentioned that the Germans blew up the extreme left of our trench, containing our bomb store and all our rations. We were next sent down to the reserve, a ruined farm house, well fortified, about half a mile behind the firing line. We remained there in comfort for the next few days. It was Thursday, July the 29th, we were relieved by the 8th R.B. We started off at 11 at night for our Rest Camp, which was reached at 3 a.m."

Here the narrative is continued from the account which Nash gave to Neville, who closely questioned him on all the points.

Nash's Account

"On July 29th when the party had marched half way back to Vlamertinghe, about 8 miles, they all lay down at once by the roadside about 3.30 a.m. About 2 hours later Nash was roused, and was told the Battn. was to return to make a counter attack on the crater, which had been vacated by the 8th Battn., owing to their being attacked by unexpected use of liquid fire. He called Gilbert, and Captn. Drummond coming along at the same time he explained matters, and Gilbert was up at once, and after the first sleepy moment was in very good spirits as they walked off after only a cup of tea — scarcely any food. Some had bits of chocolate and biscuit with them. The men knew little of what was up, but the officers knew, and talked anxiously among themselves, so that after a time the men too began to perceive that it was likely to be a hot dangerous affair. Once on the road Gilbert was consulted by the Colonel. They were to be at the W. end of the Zouave wood by 2 p.m. (on Friday 30th). The last hour or so, he and Nash walked on alone ahead of the rest — shelling became more violent as they got nearer to the wood. Gilbert said to Nash *"We're going up all together to a warm shop. I don't suppose many of us will come back"*. He was anxious lest the Platoon should not be in time, but they were on the tick, and all met as arranged — some of the rest of the Brigade in the middle, not the edge, of the Zouave Wood, and after conferring with and receiving orders from the Colonel, Gilbert went forward a little with Nash, to report about the wood. While still in the middle of the wood, Gilbert said *"I don't think the machine guns will be knocked out by this bombardment"*, clearly realizing what the probable issue was. He then was told to line up his men behind a low trench. The condition of the wood was unspeakable — trees with no leaves left had fallen from shells like spillikins one over the other, and there were

Nash's Account

corpses, and wounded men, and huge pits and horrors and desolation beyond description. They all waited from 2 to 2.40 while our side bombarded — to which the Germans answered furiously — and many were killed and wounded in the wood. At first Gilbert went up and down, cheering the men — but at last no words could be heard, so great was the noise, and he went and sat a little apart, on the right, with his head a little bent (Neville said he was sure he was praying hard, and Nash thought so too. *'He was heard in that he feared'*). He looked constantly at his watch. At 2.45 he blew the whistle which was the signal to charge — and at once the men — only 16 were now available leapt out, and rushed forward, Gilbert, followed closely by Nash (who he had told to keep near him), headed them a few yards on, with the words *"Come on my lads — this is our day"*. Soon he came to the old British barbed wire fencing, which he was beginning to cut, when he was hit in the neck, and fell over the wire fencing. Nash, badly hit in the left arm, at the same moment as his master, dashed forward, wrenched out his bandages, and turned Gilbert gently on his back, and tried to bind up the fatal wound in his neck. His blue eyes opened wide and he saw Nash and gave him a bright smile, then turned a little over, and died. While Nash's right hand was on Gilbert's breast pocket to lay him down a bullet pierced the third finger (it was afterwards amputated) and went right through Gilbert's cigarette case and, he supposed, through his heart. He crawled back, how he hardly remembers, to report what had happened, offering on arriving to go with stretcher bearers to show where Gilbert lay. But though more than one set offered to go, and two got within 10 ft. of the body, the shelling was too fierce, and after these were hit and wounded, the Colonel forbade any more going down. Some months after this Nash received the D.C.M. for the devoted care and courage he had shown.

Nash was most sympathetic for E.W. and myself, and was awfully sorry — and tears were in his eyes at the bare idea of rejoining the platoon without its brilliant subaltern, and one half of his old pals gone.

B/3484 Rifleman G H Nash, 7th Battalion Rifle Brigade
Citation for the Distinguished Conduct Medal

"For conspicuous gallantry. Private Nash, although wounded, tried to staunch the wounds of Lieutenant Talbot, under very heavy fire, and was again himself wounded. He still attended to the officer until he saw that he was dead, when he endeavoured to remove the body, but was prevented by his own wounds from so doing."

He was also awarded the French Croix de Guerre.

II. Extracts From Letters Of Gilbert's Friends

From John Murray, Student of Christ Church, Gilbert's Greats Tutor

"... It is difficult to think or write of Gilbert as dead. The volume and warmth of the life that was in him were patent to any beholder and were things for his friends to value and trust to, and to build hopes on. The fullness of effort and interest in him never failed. He had a valiant, infectious urgency, a very formidable emphasis on the *'here and now'*. There was nothing of the faint or distant or lingering about him, none of the things that make the remoteness and the silence of the dead easier to bear and grasp.

Gilbert was such a fact. There he was — present abundantly and indubitably real and significant above most, requiring to be reckoned with. Whatever he was about, he intended seriously, and his acts were full of energy. He was restless and steadfast, and both in a high degree: most himself and happiest in putting forth power.

The stricken man has vanished, but not faded or failed. His tragic end will not lend itself to pathos or sentiment, which often soften the loss of friends. It shows death at its harshest. ... He is gone, but in a triumph of life and youth, that blossomed and passed, untouched by harm or wrong. The brave memory of him has no clouds. The undiminished figure will live in many minds. His friends will possess him, for not even death can rob them of what they have known and felt the goodliness of and cared for deeply.

Gilbert was growing, and he would have continued to grow. The Army edified him and made him happy. I could see that the last time, the very last, he came to Oxford. He was bent on enlisting me. *"It was a fine life, soldiering"*, he said.

There was so much character in him that the future would have ripened a big mind in him too. He had the eye for large and fundamental things, and he faced them simply and directly. The essays he used to bring me were alike in one point — a desire to mark out the big outlines and the limits. Care for the detail would have come too, and the combination of these powers along with his gift of speech would have given him a notable place in his generation. And with his emphasis there was an intellectual sensitiveness in him that I prized, just as despite the restless force that was in him he had an unusual capacity of appreciation and admiration for others. ..."

From Victor Mallet

"It is difficult to convey an adequate impression of Gilbert as a friend and companion. A portrait in words, as on canvas, requires a touch of real inspiration to redeem it from being a flat record of outward impressions, well proportioned and accurately described, yet missing that flicker of a smile that would pass over the face, or that accent of the voice which gave point to the story. ...

Gilbert's humour was a delight to his friends. He was at his best when telling a story, and he could always convey the humour of the situation in a few well-chosen words. I remember one occasion in particular, when on a reading party in Switzerland: we were supposed to be spending a profitable evening working; but Gilbert stopped all work for the evening by retailing for our benefit the stories from Herodotus which he had just succeeded in translating. The stories in themselves were not particularly funny, but Gilbert, putting them into modern slang and pouring them forth with enormous gusto, kept us roaring with laughter for two hours. ...

I must speak mostly of Gilbert at the Chalet Reading Party, as that was the time when I got to know him more intimately than at any other time. He was at that time rather seriously alarmed about his prospects in 'Greats', and worked pretty hard. In the evenings we used to stroll round the lawn singing songs; Gilbert had a repertory of those which had to be sung with almost ritualistic regularity each evening. On one occasion Evelyn Cardew was having supper at the neighbouring chalet with Miss Asquith and her brother; Gilbert organized a party to serenade them, and a selection was rendered (in harmony) of *'I Love a Lassie'* and *'I know of Two Bright Eyes waiting for Me'*. The sickly sentiment of this latter always made him howl with laughter. ...

What he really enjoyed was a discussion of any sort. He always managed to dominate it, and yet everyone felt glad that he did, because though he talked a lot he never bored. He was particularly fond of modern novels: Wells he found intensely interesting, and Chesterton he loved. It was his power of making others listen to him that made him a leader. He could convince without resorting to quibbles or mere debating points, though as a debater he excelled.

Many people at Oxford were inclined to base their judgement of him on what they heard him say at the Union. They felt that he was the supreme debater of his time at Oxford, but did not realize the depth of thought that lay behind his command of words. But those who had the luck to hear him in small clubs or among a circle of friends round the fire, realized the sincerity of his feelings, and, even though they might disagree with his views, could never accuse him of cant. I remember one most interesting evening when he spoke to a small club on *'Modernism'*. He dealt mainly with religion and literature on that occasion (Wells, of course, was prominent in his argument) and his remarks struck me as peculiarly well thought out and full of freshness. He always gave one the impression of being vitally interested in all that he discussed. ...

There was in him much of the old conservative both in his outlook on politics and on society. His indignation at the *'Bunny-hug'* and its kindred dances was quite real, and after the *'House'* Ball I well remember him describing how he prevented certain people from dancing it! His mind, for the same reason, disliked the Land Reforms proposed by Mr. Lloyd George as revolutionary. Yet behind all his conservatism was a genuine vein of progressive feeling. He wanted reforms — many of them he clamoured for — but he loathed the idea of complete change. The world as he found it had many beautiful and dignified institutions, which he wished to preserve. His fear was that in the destruction of what was bad the good also might perish. ...

But after all it is impossible to sketch any of Gilbert's characteristics. It is useless to attempt to give the impression of that warm smile of welcome or of that vigorous body and still more vigorous mind, which made one think of Gilbert as eternally young and alive."

From A. P. Herbert

Royal Naval Camp, Blandford.
"I like most to think of Gilbert at 8 Long Wall Street, not in our happy days at Winchester nor in the great moments — and they were many — of his Oxford time, but in that last intimate year (of 1913-14) in the little old house between New College and Magdalen Deer Park, the year which ended with Schools and the War. One needed to be near Gilbert to know him, and the five of us who lived with him there, and learned and suffered his weaknesses, knew the best of him. For he was at his best as a true friend.

I see him thundering down in the morning clamouring for the morning paper, and demolishing over his coffee the latest Ministerial speech; out in the sunny garden beneath the City Wall reading Plato and talking politics; at the piano, patiently picking out some of the music he loved but could not make; swinging down the High with his ill-fated Paul behind him, many minutes late for a lecture; or up in the little room at the top of the house, surrounded by many books and heaps of untidiness, arguing far into the night with a few familiar disputants and much tobacco — always alive, always interested, always a companion.

We used to tell him he was always talking; but in truth, he never wearied us; whether revelling in a long argument on any topic from philosophy to Rugby football, or in the badinage of every day, when he would overwhelm his opponent with the rounded repartee of parliamentary phrase, at which he was an adept; passionately defending his religious convictions in some heretical and hostile club; describing with real wit some old incident of Winchester, or epitomising with huge solemnity some sermon, play, or speech which had specially impressed him — talking, yes, but we loved it.

I see him in a hundred smoky college rooms, the meeting-places of the many clubs which prized his speaking. Always he seemed to dominate the scene; usually one felt he was right. And for all his ability in public debate, it was this kind of informal discussions which most manifested his real greatness. Others might make a point, bark out a few disjointed retorts, or exhaust a side-issue, but none could so ably draw together the threads of the discussion, and with so much knowledge of political history and tendencies, and give his theme a

LETTERS OF FRIENDS

constructive and comprehensive treatment. On these evenings the rest of us, at best, were young politicians; he seemed like a young statesman. He was curiously lazy about getting up any subject involving much detail or the study of figures, Tariff Reform, for example; but in the treatment of broad questions of policy he surprised any Oxford and, as we thought, many a London speaker. We told him he might be Prime Minister, but would never make a Chancellor of the Exchequer.

Always he had the grand air; superbly brusque or even arrogant, superbly gallant and courteous, according to his pleasure. To see him at the head of his regal breakfast-parties, or entertaining a Cabinet Minister or a body of Members, was a lesson in confidence and courtliness. Yet in a great measure he was a child like his fellows, fond of simple jests and simple pleasures, excited motor-drives to Winchester and noisy sing-songs round the piano. Everything he did he did with a zest, indeed with too much zest for his success in the Schools. I remember a mock-trial being held in one of the Colleges. Gilbert, with a borrowed wig, was a perfect judge. Every little mannerism of the High Court Bench was there, the mild jokes, the paternal treatment of witnesses, the elaborate pronouncement of obvious deductions — all was portrayed to the life. Indeed, I think he secretly relished the idea of the Courts, and, if he had been nothing more, he would have been a great advocate.

I do not know what impression the above may give; but I hope it is not one of a mind devoted to the narrow circle of University politics; for indeed the catholicity of his ideals and enthusiasms was to me an abiding wonder. All the little hidden corners of Oxford and Oxford life, all the curious and interesting characters, Oxford, old and young, he knew and loved. He had views about everything and everybody, and in conversation with him the ordinary undergraduate was continually startled by the contrast which his own mind presented in this respect to Gilbert's. To his room came all manner of men — for in spite of a certain superficial intolerance, no man had a more varied acquaintance — dons, young and old, gilded youth from the House who did not appreciate his powers but loved his company, pale Union aspirants who made him their model but would never make him their companion, pure thinkers, and pure athletes, and the dark-skinned Christians whom for their faith and their allegiance he was not ashamed to respect and cultivate. One night he would be the very soul of some gay gathering, the best of young Englishmen about living, infecting all with his high spirits — and the next evening would see him surrendering two valuable working hours to attend a converted Indian's confirmation. And I am sure that he was even more concerned about the success of the Bishop of Oxford's seven-day mission to undergraduates than about that, to him immense, occasion of his Union Presidency, the visit of Mr. Lloyd George.

In grown men these may be little things; in an under-graduate they are much.

I never saw him since the War; and one wishes one had been with him in France. I know how he must have delighted in the colour, the life, the sense of adventure that belongs to the area of war, before ever the beastliness begins.

I can imagine him in the harbours, at the wayside stations, in the ruined towns, keenly interested in everything he saw, and storing up everywhere unconsciously the most vivid views and impressions; full of dry comment and his own inimitable humour."

And that perhaps is the truest tribute that one man can pay to another; that, above all, he would have gone to the War in that man's company.

From the Archbishop of York

"… Gilbert! I think of my first sight of him — a little sleeping babe in your room at the Vicarage, Leeds — of my last sight of him last Eastertide at Farnham, in all his exuberant vitality, yet with that look in his face which I now know so well in the face of boys going out to the front — the shadow of danger to come. I think of the years between — the exuberance of life and interests and ambitions becoming gradually disciplined and deepened. How could we have thought that this was to be the way in which all that abounding life was to be completed and consecrated? Sooner than we thought, and by the way of the Cross, so unexpected, so wonderful, it has achieved its noble end. In a moment, in that call *'Come along, lads'*, in that swift following call for the supreme sacrifice, accepted and followed, it was completed. Then, silence and God. Very solemn, very great. …"

From Colonel de Burgh

"In a year of sorrow and of abundant service and sacrifice, there were three men among those who honoured me with their friendship, who perhaps stand out from the rest in the similarity of their character and the fruitfulness of their short lives. They were of about the same age, they were all Oxford men, and they all died sudden and violent deaths. They were all accomplished men, with visions, such as only the young can dream. They each had their peculiarities and faults, as they were struggling each in his own way to maturity. One characteristic was common to all — they drew their inspiration from a Person, and they will all shine as the stars for ever. …

The third and last to die for England — it all happened about the same time — was Gilbert Talbot.

It would be difficult, but for that common Bond of Union, to discover ground for close friendship between persons differing so widely in character and interests.

On the one hand a boy — gay, impulsive, poetic, strenuous, affectionate, reckless even in his extreme untidiness, and immersed in political aspirations and thought, which might, had he lived, have culminated in a strong, clear-sighted and honest statesmanship; on the other hand a man prosaic, rather tired, hating politics and noise, but still alive to all the interests and strain of healthy youth.

Yet so it was. I love order; the contemplation of his writing-table at Oxford more than once caused a friendly quarrel between us, because I knew that letters must have gone unanswered. He had a large correspondence. I was impatient: until at last I began to realize that youth has not yet learned to pick up and save the odd minutes of the working day and to use time to some purpose. A man has to learn that necessity with great trouble. And anyone could see that this fault was not idleness, but the instinct of a great, unselfish, happy, loving heart, reaching out to the interests of those among whom he lived. ... His love for and pride in his immediate family was almost pathetic: the happiness of his home was a constant theme: and he was always sure of their love for and interest in him to a degree that I am not aware to have personally known of in any other case.

But Gilbert Talbot had seen the seamy side of life — and shuddered at it. He had had no time, I imagine, to see much of what we call the dregs of society, although he was quite aware that the dark places of the Earth are full of cruelty. But he had touched part of a society enervated by ease and abundance of idleness and neglecting to bring up its sons in a vivid sense of responsibility for the poor and needy. His strenuous stand for truth, honour, clean-living and righteousness, cost him to my knowledge more than a smaller man would lightly have given away, and more than quite as honourable, but less brave a man, could have endured. ...

I will not insult the memory of my friend by saying that he had no enemies. I have a pretty wide experience of men, and have never known one worth a button who has had no enemies. The slacker is always the enemy of the keen, the unclean always the enemy of the clean, the knave always that of the gentleman. ... I never heard of a coward cheerfully enduring obloquy, sneers, contempt and even persecution, with an offensive misunderstanding of his motives in high places. Gilbert Talbot did all this in his day, and the bravest thing he ever did was to go cheerfully to his death in the Army of Britain, disliking at first the demands of its discipline, and its wearisome preparation. ... And yet I venture to think, as an old soldier, that it was just this very discipline, order, and attention to detail that he required, together with the ultimate and final tragedy of his sacrifice, to enable him to attain the complete stature of his final manhood.

And so I leave my trio. The great thing is that each has left some mark on some one youth. The second of my trio was shot through the head, helping one of the boys to whom he had devoted his life, just after writing to me from his trench words such as these: *"This place is terrible Hell, but I am more at peace with God and man than ever I have felt before in my life. So long as there is but one man left in England who will help these boys in to the Light, all must be well"*. Such a man was

Gilbert Talbot, and being dead *'he yet speaketh'*.

And what he *'speaks'* to the Public School, to the Varsity both of which he knew well and to the Army of which he knew but a little, though it took his all, is this: that nothing, nothing on earth matters but to live a Life, be it long or short, strong, clean, and faithful to the Head of your Order, faithful and enduring to the End."

From the 'Westminster Gazette'
GILBERT WALTER LYTTELTON TALBOT
A Reminiscence by J. G. Swift MacNeill, K.C., M.P.

"I confess my feelings were poignant when I saw in the Roll of Honour that Mr. Gilbert Talbot's life had been laid down in the service of his country — a life which, I am convinced, would, had it been prolonged, have rendered the tides of human affairs more lustrous. I met him once only, and then but for a few hours, in circumstances, however, that strongly impressed me with his taking and brilliant personality.

So far back as November 1873 I went over from Oxford to move a Home Rule resolution at the Cambridge Union, which, to my great delight was carried. It was the first Home Rule resolution, as my friend Professor Courtney Kenny, who took part in the debate and with whom many years afterwards I sat in the House of Commons, told me, that was ever carried in England at a British, as distinguished from an Irish, meeting. In gratification of a sentiment, I asked in November 1913, just forty years afterwards to the very day, to be permitted to move at the Cambridge Union a similar resolution, which was likewise carried. The Union authorities invited Mr. Gilbert Talbot, of Christ Church, Oxford, who was then President of the Oxford Union and very noted for his intense devotion to the maintenance of the legislative relations then existing between Great Britain and Ireland, to oppose the motion. He accepted the invitation, and I met him at dinner the evening of the debate. He was a strongly built, athletic young fellow, with very refined and pleasing features and attractive manners. He reminded me, as I told him, of his father, the present Bishop of Winchester, when he was a Don at Christ Church, not much older than his son then was, and from whom I received my first lessons in English Law. I was much struck by Mr. Talbot's extensive knowledge of practical politics, his trained and wonderfully matured intelligence, and his openly avowed desire for a Parliamentary career, in which I predicted for him a success which would throw additional lustre on the record of his family, both on his father's and his mother's side, in the House of Lords and Commons.

I followed, of course, his speech in opposition to myself with an eager attention. It was admirably arranged and reasoned, and as he had to reply on the spur of the moment to several points which he could not have anticipated, I was filled with admiration at his alertness of mind, quickness of apprehension, and intellectual resources. He had great wealth of diction, but throughout, I thought, spoke under studied self-restraint, which indicated a reserve of strength to be exercised if need be. He did not fail to reply with tact, judgement, fairness, and undoubted effect to every argument. His points were always good. He never condescended to a smart debating rejoinder, nor did he ever press any argument in which he did not himself believe with an absolute and evident conviction.

He began his speech in a conversational style; his rich-toned and finely-modulated voice gave him a most favourable introduction to his audience, and as the speech progressed he rose into simple but very moving eloquence. He was throughout (with one exception) strictly impersonal. He gave his opponents credit for sincerity equal to his own. He never used a denunciatory term, although he visited certain political attitudes with grave censure. He treated his antagonists with an exquisite courtesy which was not studied but quite unconscious, the result of a charming disposition. Only once was there a personal note in his address, when, turning to myself, he said he could not but feel grieved for me in having spent my life in what he regarded as a hopeless struggle. His speech, needless to say, was a great success. I never saw Mr. Talbot afterwards, but I always looked forward with confidence to his attainment of the position in public life to which his talents and moral earnestness entitled him. As an old Christ Church man I felt proud of him as a member of that college which has given so many eminent public men to their country. Like Mr. W. G. C. Gladstone, another President of the Oxford Union in whom so many hopes were centred, he has closed a young life full of promise by a glorious death in a holy cause."

From Hermione Lyttelton

"Gilbert as a friend was all generous. All that he experienced of good or interesting or funny — and he extracted much of all three out of his short life — he brought to me. So that one might share the happiness of the experience. As his friend, one almost seemed to live with him the life of interest and delicious companionship at Oxford and in his adored home; and later in all the varied happenings of that Service Battalion training for the front.

He had a wonderful gift of narrative. Many of us try to describe incidents, funny sayings, etc., and often fail to convey either the interest or the humour. Gilbert hardly ever failed in this; he made one feel the atmosphere, and brought home to one the point or humour, whether of serious discussions or chance sayings. He got the utmost out of life, and equally he seemed to get the utmost out of people. It was a great gift of his to discover hearts of gold, or brains, or wit in people of often commonplace exteriors. He was always saying: *"Oh, he's a heavenly fellow, rather dull with most people but amazingly so-and-so when you know him"*. Whether the individual in question had character and little brain or brain and little character, or was one of the many intermediate types, he saw his point and generally made friends with him.

He was infinitely sympathetic; and in return for all he gave one, he exacted complete confidence.

He always encouraged and strengthened one; at the same time he pointed out one's faults with a truth and lucidity entirely irresistible to one's judgement: but it never hurt.

With him died to this world a combination of most of the gifts which go to make a perfect friend."

From Robin Barrington Ward, Balliol College

"Gilbert came up to Oxford a year after me, and as we were both *'interested in politics'*, as the usual classification goes, we were soon friends. A man like Gilbert was bound to be discussed a good deal in the gossipy atmosphere of Oxford rooms, and I know that I often heard him described as *'old for his years'*. This statement, to my mind untrue, nevertheless expressed a truth. It bore witness to one of Gilbert's most striking characteristics, an open, unusual and unashamed interest in all the things that mattered. But the phrase I thought fitted nobody less. Nobody could have had a cheerier, a less solemn friend. Whether he was in my rooms in the morning, twitting me with — and contributing to — the disorder on my table and the lateness of my uprising, whether we were walking in the afternoon — he and *'Benny'* (E. W. Benison) and myself — or had foregathered in Walter Monckton's rooms, nobody was quicker to see and to point out the humour of things.

Naturally I saw a good deal of Gilbert at the Union, of which we were both officers. He was keen to become President, but had the most complete contempt for the squalid intrigues that often accompany that ambition. I think it was largely due to the sincerity and reality of any views he held that he was one of the notable speakers of his time at Oxford. On his 'off' days the form of his speeches was not too good, often rather long, often a little laboured. For it mattered less to him what his speech was like than that his advocacy of the cause for which he was speaking should be effective. He never revealed himself more clearly than in his speeches. They were entirely characteristic, and — so thought one listening *'wobbler'* — uncompromisingly honest.

But largely as Gilbert's interest in politics bulked, he would discuss with you — full of the same zeal and clearness — painting, music, the latest plays, literature, religion, and cricket. I know of no one who got more out of life while he lived. Gilbert was a friend who did not forget his friends. We only met twice out here, once in Ypres, and once by a ruined brasserie when leaving trenches. On both occasions conversation started away on the old terms. Often since the day we were at Hooge, and contemporary Oxford payed a heavy toll, I have remembered and shall remember δσσακις αμφοτξροι ηλιον ξν λξοχη κατεδσαμεν with gratitude for a friendship that stimulated and lasted."

III. A Few Characteristic Contributions Of His Own

*Part of an address to the Canning Club, Oxford,
on the loss of the 'Titanic' April, 1912*

"... In the second place, while I do not wish to be melodramatic, the drama of the loss of this ship seems to me to possess a significance of the most practical kind, which should give us both some indication — if that is needed — of the state of society at the present moment, and of the direction in which it is necessary for the upper classes to move. I mean, that it seems to me beyond dispute that this giant ship was built and fitted out on a scale of luxury which is surely absolutely indefensible. Consider, in some of the accounts which have appeared in the Press, for a five or six days which are spent by these passengers in crossing the Atlantic, what are only a few of the pleasures and luxuries in which they apparently find it necessary to indulge: She had a splendidly equipped gymnasium, in which English or American millionaires could work off the effects of last night's dinner: Turkish and electric baths, probably designed for the same purpose: a beautifully designed swimming bath: squash racquet courts: several restaurants and cafes: bedrooms and suites designed in several periods, including Queen Anne, modern Dutch, Georgian, Louis XV, and Louis XVI: a machine by which those who wished could practise the bicycle: and, most notable of all, two suites for which it was necessary to pay the sum of £870 — one of the features of which was a private promenade deck which no foot was allowed to tread save that of the occupant. The cost of this vessel was nearly £1,750,000. She was 882 feet 6 inches long: her tonnage was 46,382, and her displacement 60,000 tons. This vast floating Ritz, taking her maiden voyage, was in the mishap of an instant rendered completely impotent to make any resistance against the forces of the sea. I was forcibly reminded of the scenes in the *'Last Days of Pompeii'* by the accounts you read of the last scenes on board the *'Titanic'*. Nothing in Lord Lytton's novel can exceed the dramatic qualities of the occasion: it was evening, and after dinner, the wealthy and well-dressed crowd were engaged in the vast variety of amusements which the great ship afforded: jewels, for which the Press have given various equally amazing estimates, were being worn by the lady passengers. At this moment, when none had thought of danger, and most were engaged only in pleasure, there was a shock, the obvious effects of which — we are told — were so slight as not seriously to alarm any save those actually in charge of the ship. After some enquiry as to the cause of the shock most people began to resume their pleasures, and it was not till the fateful order that all passengers should come on deck in their lifebelts was passed round, that there was any inkling that 1,500 odd of those on board were within a few hours of their death. Even then fear took some time to spread. We are told that many were reluctant

RMS Titanic

The Titanic was built at the Harland and Wolff shipyard in Belfast and was the most luxurious ship afloat when launched. The dimensions of the Titanic are:

Length   269.1m
Width   28m
Gross tonnage   46,328 tons
Top speed   43 kmh

The Titanic as designed to carry more than 3,500 passengers and the original design of the boat provided lifeboats for 4,000. The Board of Trade regulations demanded a much lower provision and it was also considered that the number of lifeboats destroyed the line and beauty of the ship. When Titanic sailed on her maiden, and only, voyage she actually had a higher provision of lifeboats than the minimum demanded.

On Wednesday 10th April 1912 Captain Edward Smith took the Titanic out of Southampton bound for New York, via Cherbourg and Queenstown. On Sunday 14th the ship received iceberg warnings were received and at 11.40pm the lookouts in the crows nest spotted an iceberg dead ahead and informed the bridge. Despite an attempt to steer away Titanic struck the iceberg on the starboard side that badly damaged the ship below the water line. Distress signals were sent out including on the new Marconi system and it soon became clear that the boat would have to be abandoned.

The first lifeboat was launched by 12.45am on Monday 15th, and like so many of the lifeboats it was not filled to capacity. Shortly after 2.00am the bow was under the icy waves and by 2.20am the stern section slid out of sight.

The RMS Carpathia arrived at 4.10am and picked up the survivors from the lifeboats. At 8.50am she set off for New York, arriving on Thursday 18th. Of the recorded 2,223 passengers and crew only 706 survived, 1,517 men women and children (or 68.2%), died.

to enter the life-boat because they thought the panic unnecessary, and the ship certainly the most comfortable and probably the safest place, comforted as they were by the confident assertion that the *'Titanic'* was unsinkable. The band, the heroism of which throughout was not the least remarkable of these events, kept up everybody's spirits by playing cheerful and attractive airs. But as the hours passed, the true gravity of the situation became more apparent, as an ominous sinking of the bows became more and more obvious. The lights of the great ship became extinguished, the engines slipped rattling and roaring through the length of the ship, and in this horror of darkness and panic there took place those heart-rending scenes of terror, heroism, and separation, of which we had such vivid accounts. Finally, the ship rearing up into the air, the Band changing from its light airs to the tune of *'Nearer my God to Thee'*, and with the Captain standing at his post to the end, and as his last message shouting through the megaphone to the crowds below the simple but surely immortal message *'Be British'* — this miracle of science and seamanship and invention and of luxury, carrying with it 1,500 lives, sank for ever from the sight of men.

Now as I have said, this disaster seems to me to have considerable practical significance. I have already mentioned the scale of luxury on which it was constructed, and I wish to refer to that again in a moment, but before doing so I should like to say that in my opinion the union of sorrow which has drawn England and America together, and the sympathy which has been extended to us by other great European nations, seem to me not mere formal expressions which have nothing behind them, but genuine signs of the attempt which is being made in every country to make a practical move towards the ideal of universal peace. There is no doctrine which is to me more damnable than that international politics are governed entirely by force, and that the morals and ideals of the nations can, when it comes to practical politics, be put out of count. That is what is called *'Réal Politik'*; a great deal too much of it is heard in Germany at present, as for instance much which General Bernhardi has just published of it is a doctrine which, if true, is a doctrine of despair. I believe that the more the voice of the democracy in each country can be allowed to make itself felt with regard to international relations, the less we shall be at the mercy of financiers and diplomats, and the more it will be found the desire of every nation is towards peaceful and unprovocative expansion. If the disaster of the *'Titanic'* can be used to stimulate this tendency, we can really say that good has come out of evil.

Secondly, it would be foolish in discussing this disaster not to notice the extraordinary heroism which was after all displayed by practically everybody on board. I would only say that the conduct of these English men and English women under such appalling circumstances is a fact at any rate worthy of consideration by those who declare that we are a decadent and moribund race.

But, as I have said, by far the most significant aspect of this event seems to me the inordinate luxury which was so elaborately constructed and so instantly destroyed. It is always difficult, and usually priggish and wearisome, to have to decide whether such and such a thing is too luxurious or not. To raise such questions continually takes life intolerable: but it is safe to say that the paying of £800 for a single suite for a five days' voyage is, without any qualification whatever, utterly indefensible and morally wrong. No really healthy individual would spend such a sum of money: that there are individuals who do it is not a symptom of a healthy state. We have all heard it said in this Club, times without number, that the greatest social reform which the Tory Party can give to the nation is a decrease of luxury and a more intimate knowledge of the interests of the working classes. That has now become a platitude. The sinking of the 'Titanic' has enormously added to its force. Of course I do not mean that the very greatest luxury is not at times justifiable by any man. What is absolutely intolerable is that this luxury should become a habit and a necessity. ..."

On Love. To a friend

"... It's always been a tremendously strong instinct with me to be afraid of the whole subject of love and to avoid ever playing with it. I should feel absolutely as if I was playing with dynamite. And then, too, I've always had another instinct which is still harder to express, but I mean a sort of idealizing of love and a terror of raising up cheap imitations, which would spoil the ideal. All this I say is a matter of instinct, not of thought or opinion. Frankly, the view of your actress friend seems to me intolerable. To have a series of pseudo-love affairs like that sounds too dreadful. And although one may not be in earnest oneself, very possibly the other person is, and then it's such desperate bad luck on him or her. It's all very well to talk about being a butterfly, or on the other hand for a man to be always making up to girls, but surely there's a very cruel element in it. And if a man or woman's life is nothing but a series of love affairs, will he or she be able to know when something different from the others comes along, and won't love be for them a thing they have made hackneyed or common by much use?

I don't think it necessarily follows that anybody who feels like that takes life seriously or has not got any amount of *'joie de vivre'*. At least I don't believe that I really take life very seriously do I? ..."

To a friend

Farnham.
July 28th, 1912.
"Neville arrived here yesterday for the week end. I have been reading with immense interest an essay he has written, called *'The modern situation'*, which is to form one of a book of seven theological essays by himself and some other young men, and is to be published shortly. His line of argument is that the change in modern thought from Mid-Victorian thought is that whereas fifty years ago there were certain assumptions about religion, morality, etc., which everybody,

On 'The Modern Situation'

of whatever opinion, took for granted and nobody disputed — now, nothing was taken for granted, and there was no principle, however apparently obvious, which some of the moderns did not question. The result was for greater confusion and controversy and a greater groping in the dark, with an almost passionate and panic-stricken search for truth, which makes some of Wells' and Galsworthy's writings, for instance, so wistful and poignant. On the other hand, because men feel their foundations much less secure, because the unrest in thought and convention is so great, the opportunity for Christianity is greater than ever before because the religion of Christ appeals primarily to those who feel the danger and perplexity more than to those who feel complacent and safe.

I'm sure the essay would interest you, because it's quite admirably written. I feel the truth of it very much. The one thing the moderns will not tolerate at any price is a formula which they are expected to take for granted. And they are so right. It is foolish to expect human nature to obey a system of morality and convention for its own sake. What a person does is always eventually determined by their personal relations. The conventions and the system are necessary for the good of society, but nobody will ever keep to them for that reason especially in any moment of crisis. Therefore the appeal of religion and Christianity must necessarily be personal. Christ does not ask that what He lays down as Christian morality should be kept chiefly because it is good in itself though undoubtedly he does say that too — but primarily because His appeal is to personal attachment and love, which is what will really direct the life of a man or a woman. And that is what I believe will be the next development of the moderns. There is a chaos at present — and what they search for is something personal."

The following extracts are from a paper which Gilbert read, as Secretary, at the Canning Club in February 1912 when he was twenty. It is customary for the Secretary to read a paper bearing on the events and impressions of various sorts during the vacation at the opening of each term, and I think, in spite of the considerable trouble involved in preparation for them, that it was a pleasure to Gilbert to deliver these papers — a sort of *'letting off of steam'* in a year full of vivid public interests.

He saw a good deal of some of the German under-graduates of his time, and in particular of a Mr. Hahm, who enlisted his help and enthusiasm in forming an Anglo-German Society — of which he said in the early part of 1915 that *"the discussions which resulted were genuine, interesting, and — in view of after events — I think tragic"*. I remember Gilbert's dwelling on the interest and pleasure of this intercourse, and when the war broke out he wrote that *"it is natural for any man, who cares for truth, to try and make up his mind what are really the rights and wrongs of this great quarrel"*.

Some will, I think, like to see how the *'German problem'* was thought about by young fellows at Oxford two or three years before this appalling war, (of Christendom), and I add a short extract on China and her marvellous development and advance, and on the problem of her position in the future.

On 'The German Problem'

Extract from address at the opening meeting of the Canning Club for the Lent Term of 1912

"... I turn now to the important and ominous situation which exists between the great Powers of Europe, and with which this country is definitely concerned. It is impossible for anybody who soberly considers the present relations between England and Germany, who is genuinely anxious for peace, and who is not swayed by mere alarmist feelings, to feel other than an intense anxiety. We are assured by Englishmen who know Germany that the feelings of a certain section at any rate of the German nation are more sinister and less conducive to peace than was the case, say, a year ago. It cannot be said that the Agadir incident and the Morocco negotiations have improved the relations between the countries. It must be acknowledged quite plainly that the German view of that episode and the English view are in total disagreement, as was shown by that most interesting debate which took place in this Club last term, and which was attended by several very able speakers from among the German members of the University. ... To preserve the peace of Europe has ever been the policy of this country; and never was it more imperatively necessary than at that moment. It is nonsensical to think that a quarrel between France and Germany is other than an European crisis which must affect every other Power. ...

The negotiations between the three countries, after passing through a period of the acutest anxiety, reached happily enough a peaceful solution; and the quarrel is at an end. But for anyone who reviews the facts in his mind to imagine that the result of the whole affair would be anything but a setback to the friendly relations of the two countries is an impossibility. The German scheme failed; they attempted, in our view, an unjustifiable policy of *force majeure*; it was England's duty, with as little provocation as possible, to see that no untoward results followed on such an attempt. The result in the German mind cannot be anything but a feeling of annoyance and disappointment. We have sufficient proof that this is the case. Any member of this Club had only to do as I did, and ask the opinion of one of our German friends on Sir Edward Grey's speech directly after it was delivered, to discover how real this feeling of embitterment and disappointment is.

But since the negotiations have come to a successful conclusion, it is now the duty of everyone who realizes what a colossal calamity war between England and Germany would be to make every effort to get the Morocco affair forgotten, and to develop a feeling of friendliness between the two peoples. In passing, I would, as far as I am personally concerned, wish to protest with all the force in my power against the view which is heard quite commonly expressed, that war between England and Germany is inevitable. That is a bit of despair and pessimism which I do not believe should be tolerated a moment. The results in loss of life and the complete disorganization

Sir Edward Grey

On 'The German Problem'

of the commerce of the two countries, and the consequent misery and distress that would be caused, should make it intolerable for war to be called inevitable. And it should be pointed out that every time that statement appears in print it is a step back in the cause of peace and a provocation in the interests of war. Mr. Bonar Law will never say a truer or wiser thing than that, if war did take place, it would not be because it was inevitable, but because of human folly.

But, for all that, considering both the Morocco negotiations and the general situation, there is cause for the deepest anxiety. Germany is beyond all doubt profoundly dissatisfied with her position in the world, commercially and territorially. She feels, as we have been told so very often, that she is a great nation, progressive and expanding, which must have an outlet for her commerce and population, and have ample opportunities for developing her genius. They are confronted with England, possessing the richest colonies in the world, and with an established position on the commercial trade routes. I don't think that any member of the Club feels any doubt that, if it is reasonably possible, German expansion should be allowed to proceed as far as may be. It is no use trying to hinder the growth of nations. Such attempts are retrograde and provocative. But the supreme difficulty is that, although the subject has been universally and carefully discussed, it is impossible to understand what the practical demands of Germany are. They are not for our colonies. Most reasonable Germans realize that for the German people (who are not a good colonizing race) to attempt to govern any of our great self-governing dominions, is a piece of the most grotesque and impossible folly. On lines of commercial expansion the problem is harder. England has not the smallest desire to prevent the expansion of German commerce. On the contrary, such expansion could only benefit ourselves. But it is impossible to allow Germany to proceed at our expense; and when such expansion is at the expense of England, it is impossible for English statesmen to consent to it. As a matter of fact, I do not believe that this clash will often take place; and I am perfectly certain that it does not account for the present state of feeling between the two countries. No commercial squabbles would account for this far-reaching antagonism, although they may have something to do with it And in my opinion the situation is most correctly described as I heard it the other day in conversation: that Germany sees England's face everywhere, and wishes to smack it! Their practical demands have never seen the light of day. Much thought and ingenuity fails to produce them. But it is clear that a general irritation and resentment is caused in the German breast by the continual prominence of England's power and prosperity.

To deal with such a state of feeling requires the greatest patience and care. There is no solution except a constant watch being kept by all who have the interests of progress at heart in both countries that no provocative action is taken, and no aggressive policy is resorted to. This must be accompanied by steady education of public opinion that on the one hand England's prosperity and greatness is not a hindrance to German expansion and German nationhood, and on the other that Germany's wish to realize her fullest capacities and her highest aims contains no peril for any part of the British Empire.

In each country there are, however, a number of persons whose attitude provides a real obstacle to a growing understanding. The existence of this party in Germany is proved by the fact that there is a definite demand for an extravagant, disproportionate, and secretly- and swiftly-built navy. The command of the sea is not necessary for German expansion: it is not necessary for German colonization. And this attempt to race Great Britain as a naval power shows (what competent observers in Germany have already informed us is the case) that there is a section of the German people whose object is aggression pure and simple, who desire to supersede England in command of the seas, and who in their hearts quite frankly would rejoice in the destruction of this country. To prevent this section gaining the upper hand must be the continued and vigorous effort of all really patriotic Germans. In England, on the other hand, there are, I believe, a mere handful of people who actually wish for war with Germany, or for an aggressive policy. But there is a section of opinion which is almost as great a danger. I mean those who take the view that war is inevitable, and who stimulate this opinion by a kind of flag-wagging jingoism which contains much sickening bravado and little or no genuine patriotism or constructive statesmanship. These opinions are sometimes given expression in the songs which are heard in our pantomimes or music-hall entertainments. In fact there is a song at this moment being given in the Drury Lane Pantomime which has received a suitable castigation from the able and unprejudiced Editor of *'Punch'*. These songs can be most dangerous in stimulating public opinion in the wrong direction, and in giving needless offence to foreigners who happen to be in our midst. I would submit that it is the imperative duty of all true Tories to do everything in their power to defeat this kind of opinion, and to persuade the people of this country that a friendly understanding with Germany, though difficult of realization, is a practicable and desirable policy. ..."

I wish now to refer to another of the events of the Vacation, very briefly, and in connection with the remarks which I have just been making. I mean the extraordinary convulsion which has taken place in China. It has been obvious for some time past to all who have given any consideration to the subject, that the vast millions of the yellow races have been beginning to rouse themselves, after centuries of barbarism, to adopt some of the civilization, thought, and methods of Europe.

We have already seen Japan become a world power of the very first importance. There has been growing also an increasing anxiety as to what will be the effect on the world of an awakening to energy of the Chinese Empire, especially when they become armed with the weapons of modern war and trained with modern strategy and skill. Partly civilized they may be: but their civilization must necessarily be their own, and fundamentally unlike that of ourselves. Moreover, the vast majority of the Chinese are not Christians; and their paganism bears

On 'The Future Of China'

practical fruit in a lower standard of morality, and at times a quite savage cruelty. What will be the effect of the movement of this people, in numbers so vastly superior to the European nations? Such questions have been asked with increasing emphasis for the last twenty years. The revolution in China, and the fall of the Manchu dynasty, has added enormously to their significance. It is impossible to criticize the events which have taken place, or to say whether or not it would have been better for China to remain under a monarchy or to become a republic. Only one who had lived for years on the spot would be justified in advancing an opinion. But what is clear is that the old government of China was corrupt, tyrannical, and barbaric, and that under it no progress or application of new ideas was possible. With a mighty effort the Chinese have thrown off the yoke. They have got a new reformed government: and the possibilities of the future are unlimited. It is quite safe to say that this event is as important as anything that has happened in the course of the last century.

What should be the attitude of Europe towards reformed China, or towards the yellow races generally, is again a question which I shall not attempt to answer. But clearly the problem before us is that some arrangement ought to be arrived at by the great European civilizations in conjunction with America, by which, in the event of the yellow races becoming aggressive, Christian civilization and progress could be defended and could survive. ... As I have tried to indicate, the question of the relations of England and Germany, the awakening of China, the possibilities of Imperial union or Imperial federation, both on commercial and defensive lines, all form part of one vast world problem which I hope may engage the attention of the Club in its various aspects on several different occasions. The difficulties resolve themselves into the following questions:

i How can an European war, which would be utterly destructive of modern commerce, be averted?
ii How can the peoples of England and Germany be brought into a trustful and willing friendliness?
iii What steps, if any, should be taken by the Western peoples to meet the new movement in China?
iv Are the present bonds of the British Empire adequate to preserve its integrity? or is it possible to change them (a) in defensive matters; (b) in matters of sentiment; (c) in commercial affairs?

Perhaps the discussion this evening may to some extent answer some of these questions."

Part II

Additional Information

Sanctuary Wood Cemetery

Sanctuary Wood Cemetery is located 5kms east of Ieper town centre, on the Canadalaan, a road leading from the Meenseweg (N8), connecting Ieper to Menen. From Ieper town centre the Meenseweg is located via Torhoutstraat and right onto Basculestraat. Basculestraat ends at a main cross roads, directly over which begins the Meenseweg. 3kms along the Meenseweg lies the right hand turning onto Canadalaan. The cemetery itself is located 1½km along Canadalaan on the right hand side of the road. 100m beyond the cemetery at the end of the Canadalaan is the Hill 62 Memorial.

Sanctuary Wood is one of the larger woods in the commune of Zillebeke. It was named in November 1914, when it was used to screen troops behind the front line. General Edward Stanislaus Bulfin (commander) ordered that the wood could not be used without his permission — hence the title, Sanctuary Wood. It was the scene of fighting in September 1915 and was the centre of the Battle of Mount Sorrel (Friday 2nd Tuesday 13th June 1916) involving the 1st and 3rd Canadian Divisions.

General Bulfin

There were three Commonwealth cemeteries at Sanctuary Wood before June 1916, all made in May-August 1915. The first two were on the western end of the wood, the third in a clearing further east. All were practically obliterated in the Battle of Mount Sorrel, but traces of the second were found and it became the nucleus of the present Sanctuary Wood Cemetery.

At the Armistice, the cemetery contained one hundred and thirty-seven graves. From 1927 to 1932, Plots II-V were added and the cemetery extended as far as *'Maple Avenue'*, when graves were brought in from the surrounding battlefields. They came mainly from the communes immediately surrounding Ypres, but a few were taken from Nieuport (on the coast) and a few from other cemeteries. Most of these burials were from the 1914 Battles of Ypres and the Allied offensive of the autumn of 1917. There are now one thousand, nine hundred and eighty-nine Commonwealth servicemen of the First World War buried or commemorated in the cemetery. One thousand, three hundred and fifty-three of the burials are unidentified. Many graves, in all five plots, are identified in groups but not individually.

Sir Edwin Lutyens

The cemetery was designed by Sir Edwin Lutyens.

No of Identified Casualties: 637

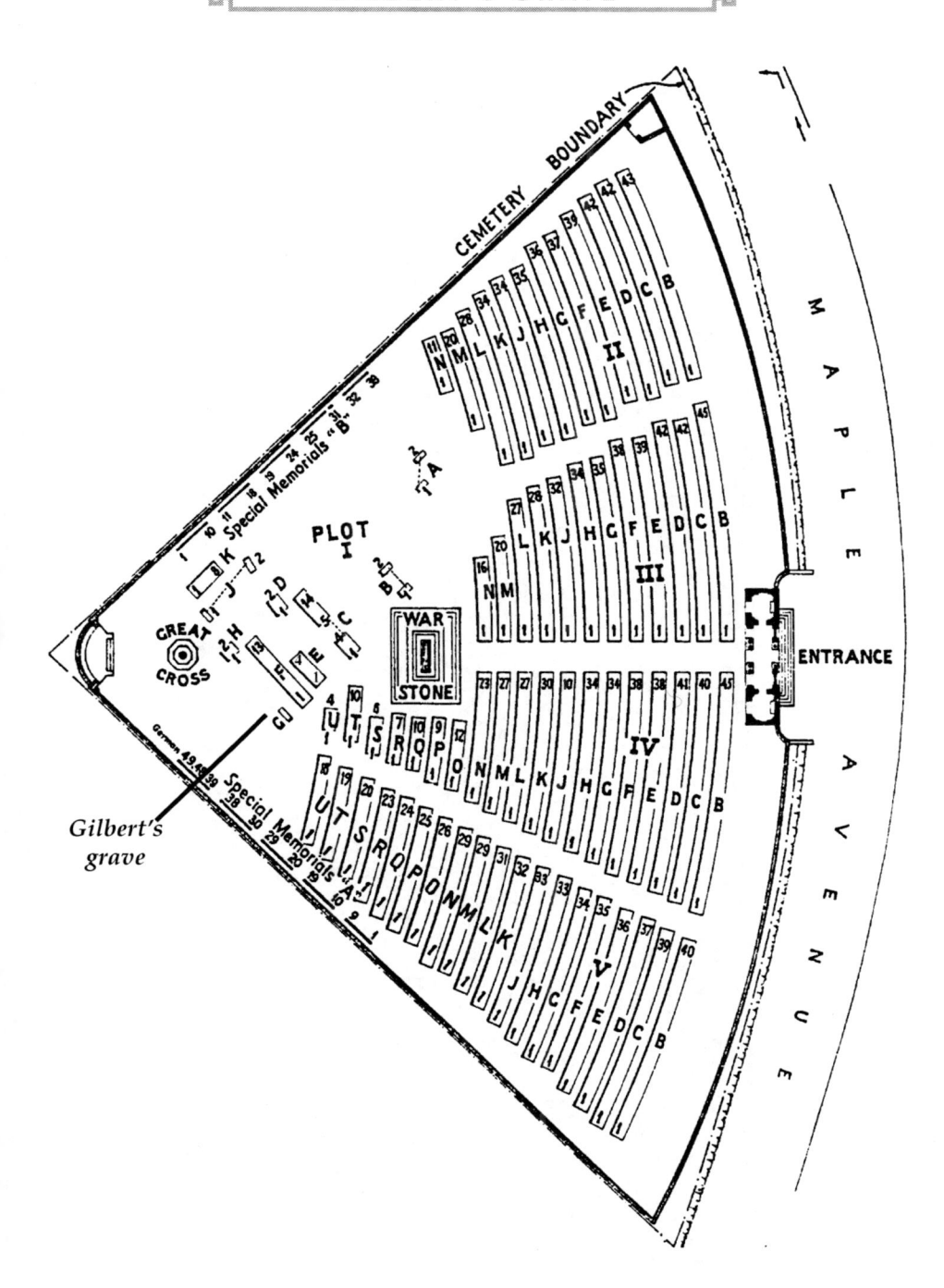

GILBERT'S GRAVE

Gilbert's grave

GILBERT'S GRAVE

LIEUTENANT
GILBERT WALTER LYTTELTON TALBOT
7th Battalion Rifle Brigade
Died on Friday 30th July 1915, aged 23
Grave reference I. G. 1.

His gravestone inscription reads:
"Fear not I am He that liveth. In lumine tuo videbimus lumen."
Gilbert is commemorated on the House of Lords War Memorial.

GILBERT'S GRAVE

*Sanctuary Wood Cemetery
and a view of Gilbert's grave, below*

Some Members of Gilbert's Family

Gilbert was born in Leeds on Tuesday 1st September 1891, youngest son of Edward Stuart Talbot, the Right Reverend the Lord Bishop of Winchester and the Hon Mrs Lavinia Talbot, of Farnham Castle, Surrey. Gilbert was grandson of George, 4th Lord Lyttelton, PC, KCMG, and great-grandson of Charles, 2nd Earl Talbot. Amongst many of Gilbert's illustrious relations is Humphrey Lyttelton, the late famous jazz band leader and media personality.

Lavinia Talbot

The Earl of Talbot's titles combined with those of the Earls of Shrewsbury, the Lords Lyttleton with Viscount Cobham.

Family coat of arms of the Earl of Shrewsbury and Talbot

Family coat of arms of the Viscounts Cobham and the Lords Lyttleton

His Father, Edward Stuart Talbot

Edward was born on Monday 19th February 1844, second son of the late Hon John Chetwynd Talbot, QC, the fourth son of Charles, 2nd Earl Talbot, and Caroline Jane Talbot, daughter of James Stuart-Wortley, 1st Baron Wharncliffe. He was educated at Charterhouse and went up to Christ Church, Oxford where he graduated with a BA in 1866 followed by an MA in 1869 and a DD in 1888.

Edward was ordained a Deacon in 1869 and priest in 1870. He was appointed the Warden of Keble college, Oxford, from 1869 to 1895, Chaplain to the Archbishop of Canterbury 1870 to 1895, commissary to Bishop of Colombo 1881 to 1891, vicar of Leeds 1888 to 1895, Honorary Chaplain to HM Queen Victoria 1892 to 1894, Honorary Canon of Ripon 1892 to 1895, Rural Dean of Boroughbridge 1890 to 1895; Dean of the Collegiate Church of St Saviour's, Southwark 1897 to 1905, Dean of Southwark

The Sees of Rochester, Southwark and Winchester where Edward served as Bishop

1905. In 1895 Edward was consecrated Bishop of Rochester and translated to Southwark on the creation of the See on Wednesday 17th May 1905, and finally Bishop of Winchester in 1911. He died on Tuesday 30th January 1934 and is buried in the grounds of Winchester Cathedral.

Edward married Lavinia on Wednesday 29th June 1870. She outlived her husband and died on Monday 9th October 1939.

His Siblings

Mary Catherine Talbot who was born on Saturday 2nd October 1875, she married the Reverend Lionel Ford, Headmaster of Harrow School. She died on Monday 2nd September 1957.

Edward Keble Talbot who was born on Monday 31st December 1877. He was educated at Winchester College from 1891 and went up to Christ Church, Oxford. He went into the church and during the First World War he served as an Army Chaplain and awarded the Military Cross. After the war he was appointed Chaplain to the King. He died on Friday 21st October 1949.

Neville Stuart Talbot who was born on Thursday 21st August 1879. He was educated at Leeds Grammar School and Haileybury from 1892 to 1899. He joined the army and served in the South African War. When Neville returned he went up to Christ Church, Oxford, in 1903. He attended Cuddesdon in 1907 and was ordained a Deacon in 1908, a priest the following year and went to serve as Chaplain of Balliol College. During the First World War he served as an Army Chaplain becoming Assistant Chaplain-General. He was instrumental in supporting the establishment of TOC H with *'Tubby'* Clayton — see below.

In April 1918 Neville married and in 1920 he was appointed the Bishop of Pretoria. He returned to England and became the vicar of St Mary's Church, Nottingham. He died on Monday 3rd April 1943 at TOC H's religious headquarters at All Hallows, Barking.

Lavinia Caroline Talbot who was born on Saturday 15th April 1882 and died on Saturday 30th September 1950, she never married.

His Uncle, General The Right Honourable Sir Neville Gerald Lyttelton, GCB, GCVO, PC

Neville was born on Tuesday 28th October 1845, elder brother of Gilbert's mother. He was educated at Eton College. He was married to Katherine Sarah, daughter of the Rt Hon James Stuart Wortley and lived at Bell Hall, Belbroughton, Worcestershire. Neville was a keen cricketer.

In 1865 Neville became a career soldier serving in the campaigns in Canada, Egypt (including the Nile Expedition) and Boer War. He was appointed Major General in 1899, and Lieutenant General in 1901.

Neville was Commander of South African Forces from 1903 to 1904, Commander in Chief of Ireland from 1908 to 1912. He was appointed Colonel of the Rifle Brigade and Commissioner of the Duke of York's Royal Military School from 1919 to 1931. Neville died on Monday 6th July 1931.

Neville Lyttelton

His Cousin, Mary Hermione Lyttelton, CBE

Hermione was born on Monday 15th October 1894, the daughter of Sir Neville Lyttelton (see above). Gilbert was close to her and as can be seen from Part I of the book as he often corresponded with her.

She served in the First World War and was Mentioned In Despatches. On Saturday 1st March 1919 Hermione married William Lionel Hichens, MA, who was educated at Winchester and became Chairman of Cammel Laid & Co Limited. He was killed in Church House, Great Smith Street, Westminster, London, on Monday 14th October 1940 and is buried in Westminster City Cemetery. Hermione became an Alderman and a Justice of the Peace for Oxfordshire and was appointed CBE in 1950.

... bombing the way forward at Hooge

From Training To Burial

The 7th Battalion was formed in Winchester on Friday 21st August 1914 and trained at Aldershot and Elstead. Once training was completed the sailed on board *SS Queen* for Boulogne on Wednesday 19th May 1915 and entrained for Watten where training continued. From Friday 28th the Battalion undertook a week of practical front line experience attached to the 5th Battalion Lincolnshire Regiment and the 4th Battalion Leicestershire Regiment. Their initial task was to supply working parties before taking the line for the first time in the Salient.

The Battalion was due to take the line at Hooge on Thursday 22nd July and relieve the 1st Battalion Gordon Highlanders, however, a mine was blown and therefore the relief was delayed for twenty-four hours. The British were not able to take advantage of the mine crater as it came under sustained attack, with the Germans pouring trench mortars, coupled with heavy machine-gun fire, onto the whole area. It was not a promising arrival for the 7th Battalion who took the front line trenches to the left of the crater and immediately came under German fire. The first task was to repair and rebuild the badly damaged trenches, and the whole night was spent undertaking that task. The next morning the Germans

... blowing a mine

blew a mine that destroyed the trenches again. They remained in the line until they were relieved by the 8th Battalion and returned to camp at Vlamertinghe. The German wire tappers had been active, carefully monitoring the telephone traffic and recording the movement of troops in and out of the line. They were well aware that the inexperienced 8th Battalion were about to occupy the line and waited for them to arrive before undertaking their attack on the British line using *'Flammenwerfer'* (flame throwers or 'liquid fire') for the first time, commencing at 3.15am (*a full description of the action is detailed below*).

The 7th Battalion arrived in camp at 3.45am where everyone collapsed onto their beds totally exhausted. After only an hour the Battalion was ordered to 'stand to' and at 7.00am they marched back along the route they had taken only a few hours previously. The Battalion halted at Ypres where Colonel Mariot-Maitland received his orders from the Brigade Headquarters in the ramparts. The Battalion was ordered to take the line where they arrived at

FROM TRAINING TO BURIAL

Above: Hooge Château in 1914

Below: A flame thrower used later in the war

FROM TRAINING TO BURIAL

1.30pm. Half-an-hour later a preliminary bombardment commenced; at 2.45pm the lead companies advanced, despite the Colonel sending the message: *"In my opinion situation precludes counter-attack by day. Counter-attack would be into a re-entrant and would not succeed in face of the enfilade fire"*. The Battalion were in support in *'Zouave Wood'*, as they advanced they found that much of the wire remained intact and the German machine-gunners on the top of the ridge at Hooge firing down on them. Colonel Mariot-Maitland ordered the Battalion to hold the line where they were.

The information relating to Gilbert's death is well-recorded elsewhere in the book. On Saturday 7th August his brother, Chaplain The Reverend Neville Talbot, arrived at the East Yorkshire Battalion Headquarters in *'Zoave Wood'* to search for Gilbert's body. Sergeant Shepherd gave Chaplain Talbot the information as to where Gilbert lay in No Man's Land, and with three other NCOs went out that night to recover his body. It was recorded: *"At the appointed time the little party stole out from the trenches and began that fearful search in No Man's Land, amidst the barbed wire and the dead. Their dim forms were silhouetted against the partial moonlight over the village of Hooge. It was a weird picture, for from their sentry posts on the outskirts of Sanctuary Wood the Germans soon detected the strange movements of Shepherd and his comrades, whilst from the sandbagged British trenches the Rev. Talbot followed the little band, his eyes fixed anxiously on the four men. A few rifle shots (without effect) came fro the German trenches and then the searchers in No Man's Land stopped. They had come to a point where lay a little group of dead. Stooping, they opened out the stretcher, lifted on to it the lifeless body of the young subaltern, and began their painful trek back again to the trenches. Not another shot was fired by the Germans until the little party had dropped safely into the trenches. On the floor of the trench the stretcher was laid down and the gallant N.C.O. and his comrades stook with bowed heads whilst the Chaplain bent over the dead body and identified it as that of his brother. Near Hooge, in the little military cemetery, the dead officer was laid to rest and, in memory, Talbot House ('TOC H') as a club for all ranks was opened on 15th December, 1915, at Poperinghe, by the Rev. Neville Talbot."*

... on patrol

OFFICERS OF THE BATTALION WHO DIED THE SAME DAY INCLUDE:

SECOND LIEUTENANT GUY FRANCIS ORMAND DEVITT
7th Battalion Rifle Brigade
Died on Friday 30th July 1915, aged 23
Commemorated on Panel 46, The Menin Gate.

Guy was born in Harrow on Thursday 28th July 1892, son of Andrew and Jane Dales Devitt, of Coldshott, Oxted, Surrey. He was educated at Marlborough College from September 1906 as a member of Littlefield, and went up to Gonville and Caius College, Cambridge, in 1912.

Guy trained at Aldershot and Elstead. He arrived in Boulogne on Wednesday 19th May 1915 and was sent to Watten for further training. Guy led his men into the line for their first tour of duty and remained in and out of the line without being involved in any major action until mid-July. On Thursday 22nd July a mine was blown in front of Hooge, Guy went into the line on Friday 23rd, the relief being delayed by a day due to the blowing of the mine. The Battalion spent their first twenty-four hours rebuilding the line that was completely undone when the Germans blew their own mine on Saturday 24th! The Germans followed the blowing of their mine with an attack that Guy and the men repulsed with support from the British artillery. Shortly before midnight on Friday 29th the 8th Battalion arrived to relieve the 7th who wearily marched to Vlamertinghe, arriving at 3.45am. The Battalion was exhausted after the particularly difficult tour and gratefully collapsed into their beds. It did not last long as an hour later they were roused. The Germans had mounted a terrific attack against Hooge, against the 8th in particular, and the 7th were needed for a counter-attack. Without food or any proper rest Guy and the Battalion returned from whence they had only just arrived. *En route*, Colonel Heriot-Maitland halted them whilst he attended headquarters in the ramparts of Ypres to receive his orders for the counter-attack.

The Battalion had left Vlamertinghe at 7.00am but did not reach their lines until 1.30pm, so difficult was their move forward during the raging battle. At 2.45pm they moved forward against the German lines. The battle was fierce, the plans were sketchy in the extreme and not well thought through. As Guy led his men forward from *'Zouave Wood'* he found the wire uncut and progress was impossible: orders were received for them to dig in and hold their position.

The ruins of Vlamertinghe after the war.
(Photo courtesy of CWGC.)

German machine-gun fire was tremendously fierce from their high position on the ridge. In the infernal mêlée Guy was killed.
In St Swithun's Church, East Grinstead, West Sussex, an altar screen was created in his memory with the inscription:
Left-hand screen: *"To the glory of God and in the memory of 2nd Lieut. Guy Francis Ormond Devitt, Rifle Brigade, aged 23."*
Right-hand screen: *"Who was mortally wounded at Hooge in Flanders whilst leading his platoon July 30th 1915."*

CAPTAIN SPENCER HENEAGE DRUMMOND
(See 'Those Mentioned In The Text' below)

LIEUTENANT JOHN HYLAND FOSDICK
7th Battalion Rifle Brigade
Died on Saturday 31st July 1915, aged 20
Grave reference I. A. 5, Lijssenthoek Military Cemetery.

John was born at Sproughton, Ipswich, Suffolk, on Saturday 2nd March 1895, the only son of Alice Anne Fosdick, of Cullenswood, Eastbourne, Sussex, and the late Frederick Hyland Fosdick. He was educated at Charterhouse from 1909 as a member of Girdlestoneites and went up to Pembroke College, Cambridge, in 1913 where he was awarded his Football Blue. In 1913 he played for Suffolk County Cricket Club in the Minor Counties Championship and in 1914 John went with the Corinthians to the Argentine.

John was mortally wounded on Friday 30th July 1915 at Hooge and died in the Field Hospital at Abeele.

His gravestone inscription reads: *"God takes our loved ones from our homes but never form our hearts"*.

In the Parish Church, Sproughton, Suffolk a tablet reads: *"To the glory of God and in loving memory of John Hyland Fosdick Lieutenant Rifle Brigade who was mortally wounded at Hooge In Flanders on 30th July 1915 and died at Abeele on the 31st July. He was buried on the 1st August at the Military Cemetery, Poperinghe, Flanders. Born at Sproughton 2nd March 1895, the only son of Frederick and Alice Fosdick."*

He is commemorated on a memorial in All Saints Church, Eastbourne.

... advance

OFFICERS FROM THE BATTALION

SECOND LIEUTENANT ALAN GODSAL
7th Battalion Rifle Brigade
Died on Friday 30th July 1915, aged 21
Commemorated on Panel 46, The Menin Gate.

Alan Godsal

Alan was born at Hawera, New Zealand, on Friday 4th May 1894, second son of Edward Hugh and Marion Grace Godsal. He was educated at Oundle School from May 1905 to 1913 as a member of Berrystead and subsequently of School House.

At the outbreak of war Alan volunteered and was gazetted on Tuesday 22nd September 1914. On Wednesday 19th May 1915 he sailed from Folkestone to Boulogne with his Battalion on the *SS Queen*. After a short period he was sent to the Ypres Salient and went into training at Dranouter. In July he was appointed Battalion Machine Gun Officer.

After a particularly difficult tour of duty in front of Hooge he was relieved by the 8th Battalion shortly before midnight and returned to camp at Vlamertinghe, arriving at 3.45am the next morning. Just as Alan and the men flopped down onto their beds the Germans launched their attack on Hooge using *'minenwerfer'* in their preliminary barrage, followed by an attack using *'Flammenwerfer'* (flame throwers or 'liquid fire') for the first time. An hour later Alan was roused and ordered to get the men to 'stand to'. At 7.00am they marched off, unfed and without any rest to return along the cobbled road to Ypres. They were halted whilst their Colonel, Heriot-Maitland, received orders from Headquarters in the Ramparts of the town. The movement out to the line was difficult and it was not until 1.30pm that they arrived at their assembly position at *'Zouave Wood'*. He led his men in the advance and was able to recapture one of the machine-guns, and was last seen firing his revolver at the enemy who were using liquid fire. He was killed when a shell burst and struck him in the face. Private Frank King* went to pull him in but was killed in the attempt, and he was subsequently buried in *'Sanctuary Wood'*. (* Private Frank King is commemorated on the Menin Gate, see below.)

Colonel Heriot-Maitland wrote: *"… quite my most promising officer"*.

A brass plaque was erected in his memory in St Nicholas Church, Hurst, with the inscription: *"In honour of our Lord Jesus Christ and in memory of Alan Godsal 2nd Lieut: and Batt: Machine Gun Officer 7th Bn. Rifle Brigade: younger son of Edward Hugh & Marion Grace Godsal and nephew of William Charles Godsal of Haines Hill. Born at Hawera, New Zealand, May 4th 1894. Killed in action at Hooge, Flanders July 30th 1915. Be thou faithful unto death and I will give thee a crown of life."*

Officers from the Battalion

Captain Ronald Montagu Hardy
(See 'Those Mentioned In The Text' below)

Second Lieutenant Frederick Ernest Marriott
7th Battalion Rifle Brigade
Died on Friday 30th July 1915, aged 22
Commemorated on Panel 46, The Menin Gate.

Frederick was the elder son of Charles and May Emily Marriott, of Cotesbach Hall, Lutterworth, Rugby. He was educated at Bradfield College followed by Uppingham from 1908 to 1912 where he played in the Hockey XI and was a member of the Running VIII. He went up to Brasenose College, Oxford, in 1912 and rowed in their IV for Visitors' and Wyfold in 1914.

Frederick was gazetted on Wednesday 26th August 1914 and went into training. In February 1915 he was sent to *'Witley Camp'* before moving to Salisbury Plain in March. Conditions in the camps were dreadful; thick mud, cold huts, and training was made more difficult due to the shortage of rifles and the lack of uniforms. On Wednesday 19th May Frederick set off for France and was immediately sent into the Salient where training continued. From Friday 28th they were attached to the Lincolnshires and Leicestershires for practical front line training. From early June he commenced tours of duty; on Thursday 22nd July he was due to relieve the 1st Battalion Gordon Highlanders, but as a result of the British mine blown that day the relief was delayed for twenty-four hours. The crater was under heavy-mortar fire and had driven the British from it; as Frederick took his men to the line on the left of the crater they too came under heavy shell fire. As soon as they arrived he organised his platoon to repair and re-dig the trenches throughout the night. At 8.00am the next morning the Germans blew a mine of their own which destroyed all the work that had been undertaken during the night. The Germans sapped towards their line and attacked, bombing their way forward. The 8th Battalion arrived during the night of Thursday 29th to relieve the 7th.

... a German dugout

German wire tappers were very active and listened carefully to all telephone communications, therefore they knew that the inexperienced 8th Battalion was now occupying the line. The German attack on the line at Hooge was ferocious and *'Flammenwerfer'* (flame throwers or 'liquid fire') was used for the first time commencing at 3.15am. At 3.45am Frederick and the men arrived exhausted in camp at Vlamertinghe. After only an hour the Battalion was ordered to 'stand to' At 7.00am he marched with his Platoon back along the cobbled road to Ypres where Colonel Mariot-Maitland received his orders from the Brigade Headquarters which were in the ramparts. The Battalion was ordered to take the line, where they arrived at 1.30pm. Half-an-hour later a preliminary bombardment commenced; at 2.45pm the lead companies advanced. Frederick and the Battalion were in support in *'Zouave Wood'* and as they advanced they found that much of the wire remained intact and the German machine-gunners on the top of the ridge at Hooge were firing down on them. Whilst under heavy fire, Frederick was killed.

His brother, 2nd Lieutenant Hugh Marriott, died on Saturday 9th October 1915 and is buried in Ypres Reservoir Cemetery.

... German limbers bringing the guns up to the front

THE 8TH RIFLE BRIGADE AT HOOGE, AND 'LIQUID FIRE'

Lieutenant Carey (later Lieutenant Colonel Carey, DSO) wrote a comprehensive account of the action at Hooge:

"*The 8th Battalion left Ypres by the Lille Gate something after 10 p.m. on July 29. 'A' Company was commanded by Lieutenant L. A. McAfee, an old Cambridge Rugger Blue, beloved of both officers and men; he was also in charge of No. 1 Platoon (we lost our original company commander a week or so earlier at Railway Wood — the first officer of the Battalion killed). I commanded No. 2 Platoon, Lieutenant M. Scrimgeour No. 3 and 2nd Lieutenant S. C. Woodroffe No. 4. 'A' Company was to hold the line on the left of the crater, with my platoon on the right of our sector holding up to the left edge of the crater. No. 4 Platoon was on my left, and Nos. 1 and 3 in a trench running parallel to No. 4's bit, a few yards in rear of it. 'C' Company (Captain E. F. Prior) was to hold the line on the right of the crater; Keith Rae commanded a platoon in this company and I'm pretty sure his platoon's sector was that nearest the right-hand edge of the crater. 'B' Company (Captain A. L. C. Cavendish) and 'D' Company (Captain A. C. Sheepshanks) were in support, in trenches at the near edge of the wood.*

I remember having a strong presentiment as I plodded up to the line that night that I should never come back from it alive; in the event I was the only officer in my company to survive the next twenty-four hours.

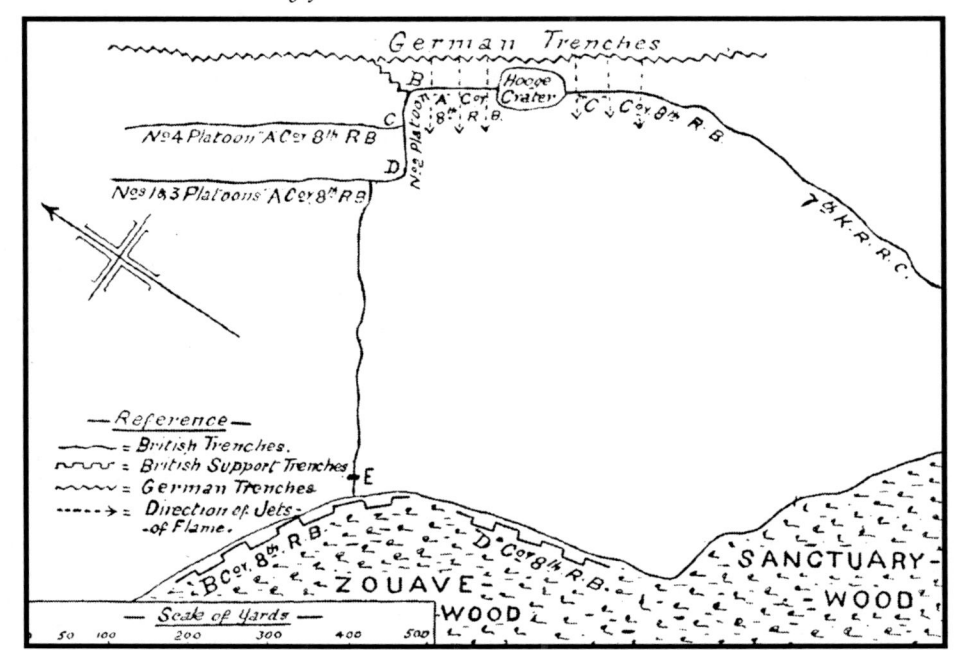

Liquid Fire

The relief was complete shortly after midnight. It has been rather a tiring business, for we had had two miles to cover before the line was reached, with the delays inevitable to troops moving over strange ground in the dark; and the difficulty of getting our men into the broken-down trenches while the 7th Battalion were getting out of them was even greater here than we had found elsewhere. I had warned my men of the need for silence, owing to the nearness of the Boche, and I remember when the time came feeling certain that the tramp of feet and the clatter of rifles must have given the show away (I need not have worried — we knew afterwards that the Boche learned from more reliable sources when a relief was to take place). Indeed, the night was ominously quiet. There had been very little shelling on the way up — for which we were duly thankful; but the absence of the sniper's bullet as we filed up the communication trench from Zouave Wood was something more surprising. The continued silence after we got into the line became uncanny. About an hour after we were settled in and the last of the 7th Battalion had disappeared into the darkness, I decided that a bomb or two lobbed over into the Boche trench running close to mine near the crater might disturb him if he were up to mischief there. (It should be mentioned here that in these early days of bombs there was only a limited number of men in each battalion who could use them, and these were organized as a squad under a single officer. Their disposition over the battalion sector and their supply of bombs was under the supervision of the Battalion bombing officer, who on this night had begun his rounds on the 'C' Company sector and had not yet reached mine. I had in the meanwhile posted a few bombers attached to my platoon at what I considered the vital spots, the point where my trench joined the crater, and Point B. Our supply of bombs was small, though more were expected to be up before daylight.) Accordingly I got one of the bombers to throw over a hand grenade; it looked to carry about the right length and it exploded well. We waited; no reply. At short intervals he sent over two more. 'This ought to rouse them,' we said; again no reply. There was something sinister about this.

It was now about half an hour before dawn, and just then the order for the usual morning 'stand-to' came through from the Company Commander. I started on the extreme right of my bit of the line, to ensure that all my men were lining the trench, with their swords fixed. Working down gradually to the Point B, I decided to go on along the stretch of trench which bent back from the German line almost in the form of a communication trench; there were servants and some odd men from my platoon in so-called shelters along here, and I wanted to make sure that these people, who are apt to be forgotten at 'stand-to,' were all on the alert. Just as I was getting to the last of these (Point D in plan), there was a sudden hissing sound, and a bright crimson glare over the crater turned the whole scene red. As I looked I saw three or four distinct jets of flame — like a line of powerful fire-hoses spraying fire instead of water — shoot across my fire-trench (see dotted lines in plan). How long this lasted it is impossible to say — probably not more than a minute; but the effect was so stupefying that, for my own part, I was utterly unable for some moments to think — collectedly. I remember catching hold of a rifle with fixed sword of a man standing next to me and making for Point B, when there was a terrific explosion, and almost immediately afterwards one of my men, with blood running down his face, stumbled into me, coming from the direction of the crater. He was followed by one or

LIQUID FIRE

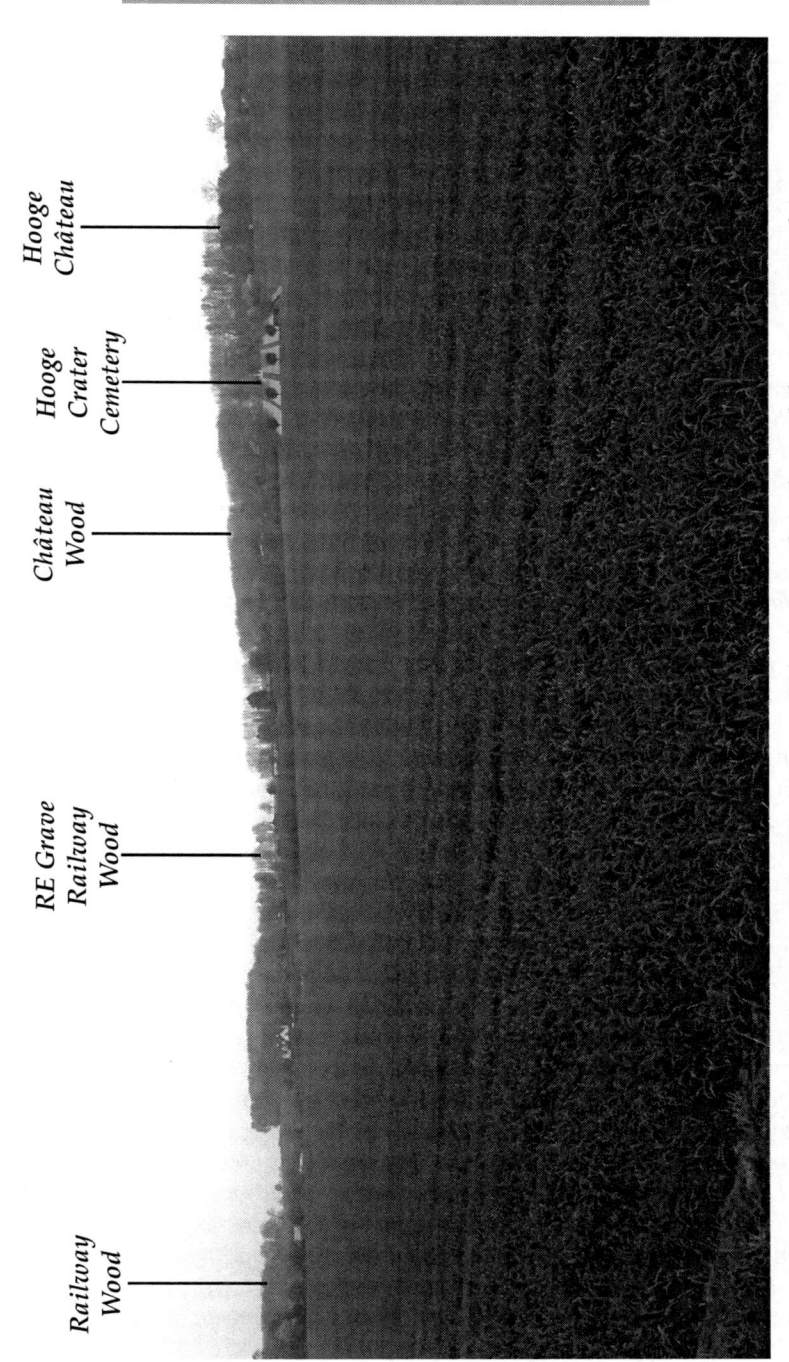

A view from 'Sanctuary Wood' looking up the slope to the ridge and the Menin Road.

Railway Wood

RE Grave
Railway Wood

Château Wood

Hooge Crater Cemetery

Hooge Château

Liquid Fire

two others, most of them wounded. The minenwerfer had started, and such men as had survived the liquid fire were, in accordance with orders, giving the crater a wide berth. Then broke out every noise under Heaven! 'Minnie' and bombs in our front trench, machine-guns from places unseen, shrapnel over the communication trenches and the open ground between us and the support line in Zouave Wood, and high-explosive on the wood and its vicinity. It was impossible to get up the trench towards the crater while men were coming down in driblets, so I got out of the trench to the right of Point C to try and get a better idea of the situation. I was immediately hit in the right shoulder by a shrapnel bullet, but I didn't have time to think much about it; still less did I realize that it was to prove my salvation. The first thing I saw was men jumping over the edge of the crater into 'C' Company's trench. It was still the grey light of dawn and for some moments I could not distinguish whether they were Boche or British; but, deciding soon that they must be Boche, I told the few survivors of my platoon, who by that time had joined me, to open fire on them, which they promptly did. At this point McAfee came up, followed by Michael Scrimgeour, and we had a hurried consultation. By this time the Boches were in my bit of trench as well, and we saw that my handful couldn't get back into it. It was a death-trap to stay where we were, under a shrapnel barrage; so Mac, after weighing the possibility of going for the Boche across the open with the bayonet, reluctantly gave the order for me to get the remnant of my platoon back to the support line, and said that he and Michael would follow with the rest of the company. About a dozen men of No. 2 Platoon were all that I could find—those who had faced the flame attack were never seen again—and we started back over the open. I doubt if we could have found the communication trench if we had wanted to, but for the moment there was open fighting to be done (we had no reason to suppose that the Germans were coming no farther than our front line). A retirement is a miserable business, but there can be nothing but praise for the conduct of the men in this one; there was nothing approaching a 'run,' and at every few yards they lay down and fired with the coolness of an Aldershot field day at any Bosches who could be seen coming over into our line. There was a matter of four hundred yards of open ground to be covered under a regular hail of machine-gun and shrapnel fire, and I have always marvelled how anyone got over it alive; as it was, most of my fellows were wounded during that half-hour's retirement, if not before, and one was shot dead within a yard of me while in the act of firing. Eventually, I (literally) fell into the main communication trench about twenty yards ahead of the support line (at Point E); it must have been then about 4.30 a.m. Here I was joined almost at once by Cavendish (O.C. 'B' Coy.), who, on learning that our front line was lost, suggested that we should there and then build a barricade in the communication trench—it was still expected that the Boche would come on. My small party set to, using sandbags from the side of the trench, and a supply of bombs came up while we were working. It was rather ticklish work when it came to the upper part of the barricade, as the Boche was using shrapnel very accurately, and there were a lot of rifle and machine-gun bullets flying about. But the men in the support trenches behind us were having a worse time, for Zouave Wood was being heavily bombarded and 'B' and D' Companies were 'suffering a lot of casualties. During this time, Mac, having got his survivors back to the supports, came

LIQUID FIRE

up to see how I had fared. He was very cool, but terribly unhappy at our losses of men and ground; and especially at having been unable to get into touch with Woodroffe. I was thankful at finding him safe, and still more so to learn that Michael also was all right. He went off almost at once to reorganize the remainder of the company. We continued to stand by our barricade, and I borrowed a rifle and tried to do a bit of sniping; the Boche could be seen throwing up the earth in our front line, and it now looked as if he were going to stay there. About this time came our first bit of consolation. Our artillery had begun to retaliate, and we could see shells bursting in our old front line; but the effort was feeble as compared with the German bombardment. Some hour and a half later Mac came back with the grievous news that Michael Scrimgeour had been killed while reorganizing his men in the wood. He also began to fuss about my wound, and eventually gave me a direct order to go back to the dressing-station. I had to go, and that was the last I saw of poor McAfee, who was killed that afternoon leading his men in a counter-attack."

Of the officers mentioned in the narrative above, Captain Edward Prior died on Friday 15th September 1916 and is buried in Bernafay Wood British Cemetery, Montauban, 2nd Lieutenant Sidney Woodroffe won his Victoria Cross in this action, together with Lieutenant Michael Scrimengeour, 2nd Lieutenant Keith Rae and Lieutenant Lewis McAfee they died in the action and are commemorated on the Menin Gate.

RIFLE BRIGADE AT HOOGE
30TH JULY 1915

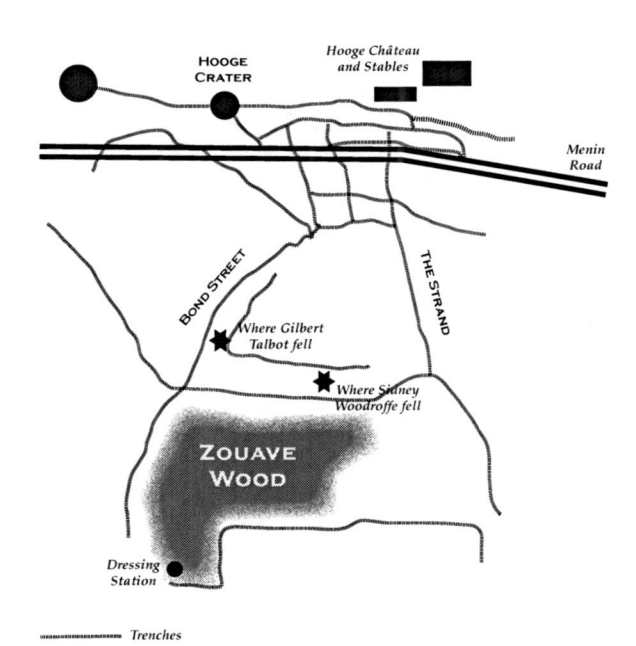

SOME OF THE AWARDS WON BY THE RIFLE BRIGADE ON 30TH JULY 1915

Rifleman Nash was awarded the Distinguished Conduct Medal for attempting to rescue Gilbert, and his citation follows the account by Rifleman Nash.

The following awards were made to men of the 8th and 9th Battalions of the Rifle Brigade:

B/1858 Acting Corporal T Brown was awarded the Distinguished Conduct Medal:

"For conspicuous gallantry and devotion to duty near Hooge during operations from 31st July to 2nd August, 1915. He carried out his duty as stretcher-bearer under heavy shell fire with the utmost bravery. On several previous occasions his coolness and gallantry have been noticed."

B/2079 Serjeant F Bunstead was awarded the Distinguished Conduct Medal:

"For conspicuous gallantry and devotion to duty near Hooge during operations from 31st July to 2nd August, 1915. He carried out his duty as stretcher-bearer under heavy shell fire with the utmost bravery. On several previous occasions his coolness and gallantry have been noticed."

S/7625 Rifleman F Hamilton was awarded the Distinguished Conduct Medal:

"For conspicuous gallantry and ability on 30th July, 1915, at Hooge. When his own machine gun had been knocked out he mounted another, the detachment of which had been disabled, and fired it at the enemy attacking from the rear. When the water failed he filled the water jacket of the gun from the men's water bottles, kept the gun in action and finally stopped an enemy's bombing attack with his fire."

B/1652 Rifleman W Hobday was awarded the Distinguished Conduct Medal:

"For conspicuous gallantry, first as a stretcher bearer, then in assisting a machine gun detachment, and finally with the bombers. He showed great bravery and coolness, and continued his duties until wounded."

B/3164 Rifleman L Schofield was awarded the Distinguished Conduct Medal:

"For conspicuous gallantry. During a pause in a counter-attack he went down the line and helped three wounded men, returning at once to his place. He did this again during another pause and finally when the attack was concluded, he crept out and brought in two wounded officers, regardless of any personal danger."

He was also awarded the French Croix de Guerre.

Awards

Captain Arthur Charles Sheepshanks was awarded the Distinguished Service Order:

"For conspicuous gallantry in a counter-attack on 30 July, 1915, when he continued to advance with his company, till only he and six riflemen were left standing. He then checked a bomb attack by the enemy, and held on to his trench till late in the evening. He was wounded in the head early in the day, but returned to duty with his company after the wounded had been dressed."

Hooge Château, an early attack on the German defenders

Information relating to some of the events and personalities mentioned in Gilbert Talbot's letters

PERSONALITIES IN THE TEXT

LIEUTENANT RAYMOND ASQUITH
3rd Battalion Grenadier Guards
Died on Friday 15th September 1916, aged 37
Grave reference I. B. 3, Guillemont Road Cemetery, Guillemont.

Raymond Asquith

Rupert Brooke

Raymond was born on Sunday 6th November 1878 the eldest son of the Rt Hon Herbert H Asquith, PC, Prime Minister of the United Kingdom 1908 to 1916 (who became 1st Earl of Oxford and Asquith, KG), and Helen his wife. He was educated at Winchester College from 1892 to 1897 as a member of College before going up to Balliol College, Oxford, where he was awarded the Craven, Derby and Ireland Scholarships, and graduated with a First in Classical Moderations and Greats. In 1902 he gained a Fellowship at All Souls College, Oxford. Whilst at Oxford he became the President of the Union with a reputation as an fine speaker and formidable debater. Raymond was a close friend of John Buchan and Rupert Brooke and was, himself, a war poet. His career at Oxford was summed up:

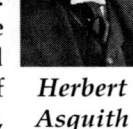

Herbert Asquith

"But the mere record of his academic distinctions give us no picture of his university life. His cleverness was so astonishing that his triumphs seemed lightly won: and indeed they probably cost him as little effort as similar successes have ever cost anyone. It was not that he was a less hard worker than others, but that his brain was amazingly quicker than theirs. His scholarship was unfailing brilliant, his intellectual interests catholic and perpetually alert, but his studies never kept him from the fullest enjoyment of the life of the university and the society of his friends."

On Thursday 25th July 1907 Raymond married Katharine Frances Horner (daughter of Sir John Francis Fortescue Horner, KCVO, of Mells, Somerset) and lived at of 17 Oxford Square, London W2 (her brother, Edward Horner, died on Wednesday 21st November 1917 and is buried at Rocquigny-Equancourt Road British Cemetery, Manancourt). They had three children, Helen born in 1908, Perdita Rose Mary in 1910 and Julian Edward George, his heir, on Saturday 22nd April 1916, who became the 2nd Earl of Oxford and Asquith. Raymond was called to the Bar in 1904. He served as a Junior Counsel for the Board of Trade during the inquiry into the sinking of RMS Titanic. Later he was appointed Junior Counsel in the inland Revenue Department. He followed his father into politics and was adopted as the Prospective Parliamentary Candidate for Derby.

Edward Tennant

At the outbreak of war he volunteered and was commissioned to the Queen's Westminster's before transferring to the Grenadier Guards the following year.

— 105 —

Personalities In The Text

Raymond joined No 4 Company, 3rd Battalion in Béthune on Monday 25th October 1915. After two weeks in billets he marched to billets in La Gorgue. Raymond's first experience of the trenches were north of Neuve Chapelle on Sunday 14th opposite the *'Hohenzollern Redoubt'*. He described the conditions in the front line in a letter home: *"I am in the trenches and have been for three or four days now, so far they are more uncomfortable and less dangerous than I had been led to expect. Waders are essential as the mud and water are well above the knee and the cold is intense. An unpleasant feature is the vast number of rats which gnaw the dead bodies and then run about on one's face, making obscene noises and gestures."* He continued on tours of duty for a week when he returned to La Gorgue. Further tours of duty throughout December were between *'Sion Post Lane'* to the *'Moated Grange'* and spent Christmas Day in the line. On Boxing Day the Battalion was relieved and sent to Merville.

Raymond left the front line to serve on the staff from January to April 1916 and was stationed at in the picturesque town of Montreuil where Victor Hugo set Les Misérables. Today a statue of Field Marshal Haig stands in the central square, an identical copy of that was placed in Whitehall.

At his own request Raymond returned to his battalion in Ap in Ypres. In May he undertook tours of duty from *'Duke Street'* to the Roeselare railway line until Sunday 21st when he was relieved to *'Camp N'* close to Poperinghe. After ten days General Lord Cavan and General Geoffrey Feilding inspected them at Volckerinchove where they trained and rehearsed for an attack on German lines. The area had been prepared as an exact replica of the ground they would attack. Training continued until Wednesday 14th June when a fleet of motor buses arrived to take the Battalion to Vlamertinghe. They took the line west of Zillebeke Lake and at *'Sanctuary Wood'*. Raymond continued to serve in the sector and in reserve on the Yser Canal, with period of rest and training in Vlamertinghe until Monday 31st July. The

General Cavan

General Feilding

... collecting the wounded

Personalities In The Text

Battalion moved south to Le Souich and spent a week on fatigues. From Sunday 13th August they served in front of Bertrancourt before being Sent for training. Whilst training in Morlancourt Raymond met his father, the Prime Minister, only ten days before he was killed. The Battalion moved to a camp at *'Happy Valley'* on Saturday 9th September and three days later marched to Carnoy. The Battalion was held in reserve when on Thursday 14th their surplus kit was sent to Méaulte and all the men were issued with their front-line equipment ready to go into the line. Raymond went with his men to their assembly positions near Ginchy and by 4.00am the next morning they sat and waited for Zero Hour. Some food and a rum ration was issued to the low rumble of slow moving tanks who were coming up to assist in the attack against Les Bœufs. At 6.00am the British barrage began and at 6.15am Raymond ordered his men to fix bayonets. At 6.20am he blew his whistle and led the first half of No 4 Company forward. As they rushed toward the German lines they came across a number of hidden Germans that opened accurate fire on the advancing Grenadiers. Raymond was badly wounded when hit by a bullet in the chest. He succumbed to his wounds at 14th Corps Medical Dressing Station. His stretcher bearers recall him giving them chocolate whilst they carried him back.

It is possible that his body could have been brought home for burial but his father knew that Raymond would have wished to be with his friends and men with whom he died. He is buried next to his great friend, The Honourable Edward Wyndham Tennant. His obituary was published in *The Times* on Tuesday 19th September.

Raymond was Mentioned In Despatches.

His gravestone inscription reads: *"Small time, but in that small, most greatly liv'd, this star of England."*

Raymond's original grave marker

Lord Oliver Chandos wrote *"He should have been spared, but he had shaken off with a shrug a staff appointment which would have made a proper use of his outstanding qualities. He returned to duty and to his brother officers with undisguised satisfaction. In him England lost one of its rarest men. Even a stranger could have see that his good looks and noble profile disclosed a man of the finest character and powers. His astringent but kindly humour many times illuminated our darkness, but with all his brilliance he was simple and unselfish enough to take his chance an make the sacrifice with men who were not his equals."*

Raymond is commemorated on the House of Lords War Memorial.

In St Andrews Church, Mells, Somerset, a plaque was placed in Raymond's memory designed by Edwin Luytyens together with his original battlefield cross from his grave. The plaque, engraved by Eric Gill, is inscribed: *"In piam memoriam Raymondi Asquith coll wintoniensis et balliolensis scholaris coll omnium animarum co socii qui in ford et republica ad omnia ingenii virtutisque praemuia spe et votis aequalium destinatus medio inflore aetatis armis pro patria sumptis fortiter pugnans cocidiit defunctum terra tenet longinqua et amica desidero in expleto prosequitur siun. VI non MDCCCLXXVIIi ob XV Sept MCMXVI."*

The Celtic cross reads: *"In loving memory Lieut. Raymond Asquith 3rd Battn. Grenadier Guards died of wounds."*

A plaque in his memory was also erected in Amiens Cathedral with the inscription: *"Priez pour l'âime de Raymond Asquith Lieuenant Aux Granadiers de la Gare Royale. Fils ainé de Herbert Henry Asquith premier ministre du Royaume Uni. Né le 6 Nov. 1878. Tombé au champ d'honneur près de Guinchy le 15 Sept. 1916*

O oriens splendor lucis æternæ veni et illumina sedentes in tenebris et umbra motis. Gloriæ memor posuit conjux."

> *Liquid fire and poison gas*
> *Leave the German where he was.*
> *Obviously, if we can,*
> *We must find a bolder plan.*
> *Why not then invoke the Muse?*
> *Surely conscience bids us use*
> *(Since we're fighting for the Right)*
> *Every form of Schreklichkeit.*
> *Then, I ask you, why not try*
> *The magic power of poesy?*
> *After all the thing's been done;*
> *Goethe was a bloody Hun.*
> *Why not in the last resort*
> *Versify the Train Report?*
> *I know it's going rather far,*
> *But — anything to win the war.*

PERSONALITIES IN THE TEXT

ARTHUR JAMES BALFOUR
1ST EARL OF BALFOUR, KG, OM, PC, DL

Arthur Balfour and his coat of arms

Arthur Balfour was born on Tuesday 25th July 1848, eldest son of James Maitland Balfour, MP, and Lady Blanche Mary Harriet Gascoyne-Cecil (daughter of James, 2nd Marquess of Salisbury). He was named Arthur after his godfather, the Duke of Wellington. Arthur was educated at Eton College and went up to Trinity College, Cambridge.

Arthur was first elected to Parliament in 1874 as the Conservative Member of Parliament for Hertford. In 1878 his uncle, Robert, Lord Salisbury (later Prime Minister), appointed him his Private Secretary. He served as Member of Parliament for the East Manchester constituency from 1885 to 1906. In 1886 Arthur became Secretary for Scotland and joined the Cabinet before becoming Chief Secretary for Ireland. In 1891 he became First Lord of the Treasury (the last time the appointment was made before the post was incorporated with the that of the Prime Minister) and the Leader of the House of Commons. After serving at the Foreign Office he succeeded his uncle as Prime Minister in July 1902. Arthur continued to serve as Prime Minister until December 1905 when the Liberals gained power. Despite losing his own seat in the House of Commons he continued to lead the Conservative Party. He was elected as the Member of Parliament for the City of London until 1911 when Bonar Law took over. Following the resignation of Winston Churchill Arthur became First Lord of the Admiralty, and under Lloyd George, the Foreign Secretary, serving until 1919. He retired in 1922 from the House of Commons when he was created the 1st Earl of Balfour. He died on Wednesday 19th March 1930.

SECOND LIEUTENANT ERIC WILLIAM BENISON
Royal Garrison Artillery
Died on Friday 13th August 1915
Grave reference C. 9. 4821, Wimborne Minster Cemetery

Eric was born in 1889, son of the Reverend Ernest Dewes Benison, MA, and Mrs Jessie Benison. He was educated at Sherborne School from 1903 to 1908 as a member of School House and went up to Magdalen College, Oxford, graduating with a BA. Eric was commissioned in March 1915. He died of peritonitis in Weymouth contracted on active service.

Eric Benison's family coat of arms

Personalities In The Text

Hubert Murray Burge, GCVO
Bishop of Southwark

Hubert was born on Saturday 9th August 1862, son of the Reverend and Mrs M R Burge. He was educated at Bedford Grammar School and at Marlborough College from 1876 to 1877 as a member of Littlefield and went up to University College, Oxford. He became a Fellow and Dean of University College before being appointed Headmaster of firstly Repton and then Winchester College. His main interest and pleasure was cricket.

The coat of arms of the Sees of Southwark and Oxford

In 1911 Hubert was appointed the Bishop of Southwark before becoming Bishop of Oxford in 1919. He was the Chancellor of the Most Noble Order of the Garter and Sub-Prelate of the Order of St John of Jerusalem. Hubert died on Thursday 11th June 1925 at Cuddesdon Palace, Wheatley.

Captain Spencer Heneage Drummond
7th Battalion Rifle Brigade
Died on Friday 30th July 1915, aged 31
Commemorated on Panel 46, The Menin Gate.

Spencer was born on Tuesday 12th August 1884, third child and second son of Captain Algernon Heneage and Mrs Margaret Elizabeth Drummond, of Preston House, Colebrook Street, Winchester and was related to the Earls of Perth. His brother, Lieutenant Commander Geoffrey Heneage Drummond, won the Victoria Cross at Ostend in May 1918.

Spencer arrived in Boulogne on Wednesday 19th May 1915 and was sent to northern France. After a period of training he was sent into the line. On Friday 23rd July the Battalion relieved the Gordon Highlanders in the line at Hooge after

Geoffrey Drummond, VC

the mine had been blown. As they arrived the Germans were bombarding the line and the newly created crater. The next day the Germans blew a mine of their own, to the left of the British one, and commenced to sap towards the British line. The British artillery opened up and Spencer, with his men, counter-attacked with bombs and the German attack was repulsed. The 8th Battalion came up to relieve the 7th during the night of Thursday 29th, arriving in camp at Vlamertinghe at 3.45am. After only an hour orders were given for the men to 'stand to' and at 7.00am they wearily marched back towards Ypres. The Germans had launched an attack on the lines they had so recently left where *'Flammenwerfer'* (flame throwers

Personalities In The Text

or 'liquid fire') was used for the first time. They halted near the Asylum whilst their Colonel, Heriot-Maitland, went to the Ramparts to received his orders. The Battalion was to support the 8th Battalion in a counter-attack that was to commence with an artillery barrage at 2.00am, and forty-five minutes later the advance. It took until 1.30pm before the Battalion reached *'Zouave Wood'*. The Brigade Commander wrote: *"In my opinion situation precludes counter-attack by day. Counter-attack would be into a re-entrant and would not succeed in face of enfilade fire."* As Spencer led his men forward from *'Zouave Wood'* they found that the wire was uncut and came under heavy machine-gun fire. In the early stages of the move forward Spencer was shot and killed.

Spencer was recorded in Debretts Obituary — War Roll of Honour published in the 1921 edition.

Second Lieutenant
The Hon Gerald William Grenfell
(known as 'Billy')
8th Battalion Rifle Brigade
Died on Friday 30th July 1915, aged 25
Commemorated on Panel 46, The Menin Gate.

Billy at School

Billy Grenfell, family coat of arms

Billy was born on Saturday 29th March 1890, son of William Henry, 1st Baron Desborough, KG, GCVO, and Ethel Anne Priscilla, Lady Desborough (Lady of the Bedchamber to HM the Queen), of Taplow Court, Clivedon Road, Taplow, Buckinghamshire, grandson of John, 11th Earl of Westmorland.

He was educated at Summer Fields from 1899 where he was a good athlete and held four School records. He then attended Eton College from 1903 to 1909 where he won an entrance Scholarship and the Newcastle Scholarship (one of the few Oppidans to be so awarded) as a member of Mr Arthur Christopher Benson's and Mr Arthur Murray Goodhart's Houses. He was one the editors of the *'Eton College Chronicle'* from 1907 to 1909. Billy went up to Balliol College, Oxford, in 1909, and was awarded the Craven Scholarship in 1911. He won a Real Tennis Blue and boxed for the College. Billy had intended to read for the Bar but the war intervened.

Lord Desborough

'INTO BATTLE'
JULIAN GRENFELL

"The naked earth is warm with spring,
And with green grass and bursting trees
Leans to the sun's gaze glorying,
And quivers in the sunny breeze;
And Life is Colour and Warmth and Light,
And a striving evermore for these;
And he is dead who will not fight;
And who dies fighting has increase.

The fighting man shall from the sun
Take warmth, and life from the glowing earth;
Speed with the light-foot winds to run,
And with the trees to newer birth;
And find when fighting shall be done,
Great rest and fulness after death.

All the bright company of Heaven
Hold him in their high comradeship,
The Dog Star, and the Sisters Seven,
Orion's Belt and Sworded Hip.

The woodland trees that stand together,
They stand to him each one a friend,
They gently speak in the windy weather,
They guide to valley and ridges' end.

The kestrel hovering by day
And the little owls that call by night,
Bid him be swift and keen as they,
As keen of ear, as swift of sight.

The blackbird sings to him, 'Brother, brother,
If this be the last song you shall sing,
Sing well, for you may not sing another;
Brother, sing.'

In dreary, doubtful, wiling hours,
Before the brazen frenzy starts,
The horses show him nobler powers;
O! patient eyes, courageous hearts

And when the burning moment breaks,
And all things else are out of mind,
And only Joy of Battle takes
Him by the throat, and makes him blind

Through joy and blindness he shall know,
Not caring much to know, that still
Nor lead nor steel shall reach him, so
That it be not the Destined Will.

The thundering lines of battle stands,
And in the air Death moans and sings;
But Day shall clasp him with strong hands,
And Night shall fold him in soft wings."

Personalities In The Text

Billy volunteered at the outbreak of war and was gazetted on Saturday 12th September 1914. He was sent for training until Saturday 22nd May 1915 when he sailed for France. He entrained for Watten in northern France to continue training; from Friday 28th he was attached to the North and South Staffordshires for training in the front line on the French-Belgian border. On Saturday 29th Major Billy Congreve, VC, DSO, MC, wrote: *"I rode off to look for Ronnie who is now out here commanding the 8th Battalion which is in the 14th Division. Eventually found him in a farm between Neuve Eglise and Bailleul. I much admired the general appearance of the good riflemen. They may be new but they look splendid and have such a fine lot of officers."* (Major Congreve was killed on Thursday 27th July 1916 and is buried in Corbie Communal Cemetery Extension.)

Billy Congreve

On Monday 7th June Billy went into the line for the first time at St Eloi for a three day tour of duty after which they were relieved by the 7th Battalion. On Monday 5th July the Germans bombarded their lines and twenty of them managed to enter the trenches. The North Staffordshire's Bombing Officer rushed in and helped mount the counter-attack which cleared them out. On Friday 30th July Billy was leading his troops from a trench in *'Zouave Wood'*, near Hooge, at 3.00pm when he was killed by machine-gun fire. He spoke to the men of his platoon and urged them: *"Remember, you are Englishmen. Do nothing to dishonour that name."* Due to the fierce battle that raged, Billy's body was not recovered until Sunday 15th August when it was buried but the grave was subsequently lost. He had written: *"Death is such a frail barrier out here that men cross it smilingly and gallantly every day."*

Captain A C Sheepshanks wrote: *"He died splendidly leading his men over open ground up hill in the face of a tremendous fire from machine-guns. His Platoon Sergt. saw him pitch forward with a bullet in the head, and thinks he was hit again in the side as he fell. He must have been killed instantaneously as he was not seen to move afterwards. Both as his company commander and his friend I shall miss him enormously. His platoon all loved him, and he had somehow inspired them with a fighting spirit, and it was only a few days ago that I told the Col. that Bill's platoon was the best fighting platoon I had."*

On Saturday 31st July, Lieutenant Colonel Alexander Maclachlan*, Commander of the 8th Battalion, wrote to Lord Desborough: *"Billy was killed yesterday afternoon about 3.00pm when gallantly charging over the open at the head of his men. It is all too tragic and I dare not think what this double shock can mean to you."* (*Lieutenant Colonel Maclachlan was killed and is buried in Savy British Cemetery.)

Billy had been killed less than a mile away from where his brother, Julian, had been fatally injured. Billy was one of the war poets.

Billy is commemorated on the House of Lords War Memorial.

At Taplow Court a sculpture of Apollo in his chariot of the sun, placed on a boulder, with an inscription that reads: *"In memory of the happy lives of Julian Henry Francis Grenfell Captain Royal Dragoons, died of wounds at Boulogne May 26th 1915 aged 27, and of Gerald William Grenfell, Second Lieutenant Rifle Brigade killed*

leading a charge near Hooge July 30th 1915, aged 25."
The associated plaque has *'Into Battle'*, composed by Julian Grenfell, inscribed on it.
His brother, Captain Julian Grenfell, died on Wednesday 26th May 1915 and is buried in Boulogne Eastern Cemetery and his cousins Captain Francis Grenfell, VC, is buried in Vlamertinghe Cemetery and Captain Riversdale Grenfell died on Friday 4th September 1914 and is buried in Vendresse Churchyard.

Julian and Francis Grenfell

'Julian Grenfell: his Life and the Times of his Death 1888-1915', was published by Weidenfeld & Nicolson, London 1976 also records a lot of information about Billy. The comedienne and actress Joyce Grenfell was related to the family

Captain Ronald Montagu Hardy
'D' Company, 7th Battalion Rifle Brigade
Died on Friday 23rd July 1915, aged 33
Commemorated on Panel 46, The Menin Gate.

Ronald was born at Danehurst, Sussex, on Tuesday 12th April 1892, the youngest son of Herbert and A Louisa C Hardy, of Chilworth Manor, Surrey. He was educated at Eton College, a member of Mr Edward Compton Austen Leigh's House, leaving in 1890.
At the outbreak of war Ronald volunteered and enlisted in the Territorials, Sussex Regiment. He was gazetted in October 1914 to the Rifle Brigade and promoted Temporary Captain in November.
After training, on Thursday 20th May 1915 Ronald sailed from Folkestone to Boulogne with his Battalion on *SS Queen*. He was sent to northern France for further training. After a week placed with the Lincolnshire and Leicestershires for front line experience, he was sent into the line at St Eloi on Monday 7th June. For the next month he undertook tours of duties without particular incident until Monday 5th July when his line was attacked following an artillery bombardment. A group of twenty German infantry managed to break into their line, however, the North Staffordshires who were next to them came to the rescue and bombed the attackers out of the trenches. Life returned to 'normal' tours of duties for the next two weeks. He was due to relieve the Gordon Highlanders on Thursday 22nd, however, during the day the British blew a mine at Hooge and therefore it was a further twenty-four hours before Ronald reached the line close to the newly created crater. He arrived under a heavy barrage and was organising his men in the line when he was killed.
Ronald is commemorated on Danehill War Memorial, Sussex.
In All Saints Church, Danehill, East Sussex, a white stone statue of a knight

holding a sword was placed in the Lady Chapel with the inscription: *"In memory of Roland Montagu Hardy, Captain in The Rifle Brigade, killed in action at Hooge, Flanders, on July 23rd 1915."*
His cousin, Captain Alfred Garthorne-Hardy, is commemorated on Loos Memorial, and Lieutenant Alan Hardy is buried in Chilham (St Mary) Churchyard.

COLONEL
JAMES DALGLEISH HERIOT-MAITLAND, CMG, DSO

James was born on Wednesday 21st January 1874, eldest son of the late Major General James Makgill Heriot-Maitland, KCB, and Lady Frances Lorna Campbell. He was educated at Wellington College from 1887 and passed into RMC Sandhurst in 1891. In August 1903 James married Mary Turner (née Wedderburn) and they had a son, Richard and two daughters, Katharine Lorna and Margaret. The family lived at the White House, Aros, Isle of Mull.

James was gazetted on Wednesday 5th October 1892, promoted to Lieutenant on Monday 24th June 1895, Captain on Saturday 3rd February 1900, Adjutant from Wednesday 21st November 1900 to Friday 2nd September 1904, and Adjutant of the Depôt from Wednesday 16th May 1906 to Saturday 15th May 1909, Major Wednesday 1st December 1909, Lieutenant Colonel on Tuesday 15th June 1915, Temporary Brigadier General on Thursday 31st August 1916 and Colonel on Sunday 15th June 1919.

... in action in the South African War

He served in the South African War where he received the Queen's Medal with four clasps and the King's Medal with two clasps. He was awarded the Distinguished Service Order that was gazetted on Friday 19th April 1901 *"In recognition of services during the operations in South Africa"*.
Following the outbreak of war James was appointed to command the 7th Battalion, Rifle Brigade.
From Friday 1st September 1916 to Saturday 9th November 1918 he commanded the 98th Infantry Brigade, being appointed a CMG in 1916. He returned to England where he took command at Bordon from Tuesday 14th January 1919.
James was Mentioned in Despatches four times.

PERSONALITIES IN THE TEXT

CANON HENRY SCOTT HOLLAND

Henry was born in Ledbury on Wednesday 27th January 1847 and was educated at Eton College then went up to Oxford. He was a Fellow of Christ Church and in 1884 became Canon of St Paul's Cathedral. In 1910 he was appointed Regius Professor of Divinity at Oxford.

Henry died on Sunday 17th March 1918 and is buried in All Saints Church, Cuddesdon.

He was particularly well-known for the following poem:

Canon Holland

DEATH IS NOTHING AT ALL

Death is nothing at all.
I have only slipped away into the next room.
I am I and you are you.
Whatever we were to each other, that we still are.

Call me by my old familiar name.
Speak to me in the easy way which you always used.
Put no difference in your tone.
Wear no forced air of solemnity or sorrow.

Laugh as we always laughed at the little jokes we enjoyed together.
Play, smile, think of me, pray for me.
Let my name be ever the household word that it always was.
Let it be spoken without affect, without the trace of a shadow on it.

Life means all that it ever meant.
It is the same that it ever was.
There is absolutely unbroken continuity.
Why should I be out of mind because I am out of sight?

I am waiting for you,
for an interval,
somewhere very near,
just around the corner.

All is well.

PERSONALITIES IN THE TEXT

GENERAL SIR ARCHIBALD HUNTER, GCB, GCVO, DSO

Archie Hamilton

Archie was born on Saturday 6th September 1856. He was educated at Glasgow Academy and passed into RMC Sandhurst.

He was gazetted on Saturday 13th June 1874 to the 4th The King's Own Regiment, then joined the Royal Lancaster Regiment, promoted to Lieutenant and was Adjutant from Tuesday 20th April 1880 to Wednesday 11th November 1882, and Captain on Thursday 3rd August 1882. Archie was employed by the Egyptian army from Thursday 28th February 1884 to Wednesday 19th January 1887 and again from Sunday 11th March 1888 to April 1899.

Archie served in the Sudan Expedition, 1884 to 1885, where he was Mentioned in Despatches, received the Medal with Clasp, the Bronze Start and the Order of Osmanieh, 4th Class. Archie served in the Sudan in 1885, 1886 and 1889 and was Mentioned in Despatches, received the Order of Medjidie, 3rd Class and was awarded the Distinguished Service Order, gazetted on Friday 26th November 1886 *"For action at Ginniss"*. He was wounded at Toski and was again Mentioned in Despatches. He was promoted to Major on Wednesday 15th June 1892 and appointed Governor of the Red Sea Littoral from Thursday 11th August 1892 to Saturday 28th July 1894. Archie became Governor of the Frontier and Commandant of the Field Force, Egypt from Sunday 29th July 1894 to Monday 30th November 1896. He took his men to Dongola in 1896 where he was Mentioned in Despatches and received the Medal and the Egyptian Medal with two clasps. He was promoted Major General on Wednesday 18th November 1896. From Tuesday 1st December 1896 to Thursday 6th April 1899 he was Governor of Dongola Province and went on the Nile Expedition in 1897 where he was Mentioned in Despatches and was raised to the 2nd Class of the Order of Osmanieh and received two clasps to the Egyptian Medal. Following Khartoum he was again Mentioned in Despatched and awarded the KCB. Archie went to India in 1899 then served as Chief of Staff in South Africa being promoted Lieutenant General on Tuesday 6th March 1900. During the South African War he was Mentioned in Despatches four times and received the Queens Medal with six clasps. He returned to England where he served until 1903 when he returned to India as General Officer Commanding of the Southern Army, from Friday 30th October 1903 to Thursday 29th October 1908. He was raised to General on Friday 8th December 1905. Archie was appointed Governor and Commander-in-Chief of Gibraltar from Friday 30th September 1910 to Tuesday 1st July 1913. He was created GCB in 1911 and GCVO in 1912. He was appointed Commander of the Aldershot Training

Cartoon of Archie Hunter as Governor in Egypt

Centre from Sunday 23rd August 1914.
Archie became a Coalition Unionist Member of Parliament for Lancaster in 1918, retiring in 1922.
On Tuesday 1st November 1910 he married Lady Mary, widow of George, 2nd Baron Iverclyde; Archie died in 1936.

Captain The Honourable
Edward James Kay-Shuttleworth
7th Battalion Rifle Brigade and Staff Captain, 218th Infantry Brigade
Died on Tuesday 10th July 1917, aged 27
Grave reference In North-East corner,
Barbon (St Bartholomew) Churchyard, Westmorland

Edward Kay-Shuttleworth and his family coat of arms

Ted was born on Saturday 15th March 1890, the youngest son of 1st Baron Shuttleworth (Ughtred James Kay-Shuttleworth MP, Parliamentary Secretary of the Admiralty) of Gawthorpe Hall (now a National Trust property). The family seats were Gawthorpe Hall, Burnley and Barbon Manor, Kirkby Lonsdale. He was the grandson of Sir James Phillips Kay-Shuttleworth (1804-1877), the educational and social reformer and of Sir Woodbine Parish, KCH.

Ted was educated at Eton College as a member of Reverend Henry Thomas Bowlby's House before going up to Balliol College, Oxford, in 1908 where he graduated with a BA in History with Honours. He was called to the Bar in 1912. Ted married Sibell Eleanor Maud on Saturday 5th December 1914 (who remarried and became the Honourable Mrs Charles Frederick Lyttleton), they had two children:

Pamela Catherine Mabell, born on Friday 17th September 1915, she married four times and died in 1972;

Charles Ughthred John on Sunday 24th June 1917, who was educated at Eton College and went up to Magdalene College, Cambridge. He served in the Second World War, won the Military Cross in 1940 was wounded twice and invalided home. Charles became 4th Baron, inheriting the title from his cousin.

At the outbreak of war Ted joined the Battalion in Churn where he was commissioned on Thursday 20th August 1914, promoted to Lieutenant in April 1915, and Captain in July 1915. He was appointed Staff Captain of the 218th Infantry.

He left for France in May 1915 and undertook final training visiting the trenches

PERSONALITIES IN THE TEXT

for practical instruction from experienced officers. In June Ted crossed into Belgium and sent to camp near Dickebusch where on Thursday 10th they relieved the colleagues from the 8th Battalion at St Eloi. After a number of tours of duty he moved into the Salient itself, to Hooge. Ted took his men to relieve the Gordon Highlanders at *'Railway Wood'* just a the mine was blown at Hooge. Late on Thursday 29th the 8th Battalion arrived to relieve the 7th. The Germans had been tapping the British telephones and were well aware of who was in the line thus prepared their attack to coincide with inexperienced troops occupying the front line on Friday 30th. Ted and his men were safely back in camp at Vlamertinghe as the German launched their fearsome attack. For the first time *'liquid fire'* (flammenwerfer) was used and the British line was pushed back. Ted had only arrived in camp at 3.45am but an hour later orders were received to stand to. At 7.00am the Battalion marched back along the pavé to Ypres Asylum where they waited for final instructions. At 2.00pm a bombardment would begin on the German positions with a counter-attack to begin at 2.45pm although the Brigade Commander considered the idea was futile. As Ted went forward from *'Zouave Wood'* the British wire remained intact which slowed them down and they came under heavy fire from the German machine-gunners. The Germans mounted a further counter-attack but that was successfully repulsed. Ted was the only officer from the Battalion to escape unscathed which caused him great upset and guilt.
Ted continued to serve in the Salient until the early February 1916 when the Battalion marched to Cassel where the Battalion was reorganised with two weeks of training. They entrained for the Somme but after arriving in Amiens they received orders to march to Arras where they took the line. Ted was injured in March 1916 and invalided home then went on a Staff course in England.
He was accidentally killed while returning to duty on a motorcycle on Tuesday 10th July 1917.
Ted was Mentioned in Despatches.
Father Ronald Knox wrote of him: *"If it is right to pay some tribute to the gallant dead, those especially who youthfulness has left behind them no monument to keep them in men's remembrance, by trying to reconstruct in words the picture of what they were, certainly Ted Shuttleworth deserves such a memorial, as certainly it seems a hopeless task to attempt it. The vivid impression he made in life is not one that can be translated into phrases besides it was full of half-truths. A casual acquaintance might think him frivolous — yet he felt deeply and puzzled furiously languid — yet he was physically strong and fond of his own strength ; impulsive — yet his nature had an extraordinary reserve of self-control. In fact his outward qualities were the first that attracted you, only to prove, when you knew him better, no part of his true self.*
Perhaps his most remarkable quality was an extraordinary purity of nature which enabled him to plunge with apparent recklessness into any society or any amusement and yet come out heart-whole — Hippolytus in Pavia. Not that he courted adventures. They seemed to court him, and found him marble. The truth was (a simple and old-fashioned truth) that the passionate element in his nature had poured itself out into a singularly strong mould of religion.

Illness delayed and the war cut short his career ; but his friends (and his was a rare friendship) knew enough of him to know that we lost in him a valuable citizen, a fascinating companion, and a devout servant of God. The tragedy of his death by an accident, after all the horrors of war he had been through, does not tarnish for them the brightness of his sacrifice or separate him in death from Torn Gent, Billy Grenfell, Gilbert Talbot, and his other friends in the Brigade who — 'terque quaterque beati' — fell at Hooge in the first battle of Kitchener's Armies."

Ted is commemorated on the House of Lords War Memorial.

"Life And Work Of Sir James Kay-Shuttleworth" (Cedric Chivers, Bath, 1974 a reprint of the 1932 original).

James Kay-Shuttleworth: "Journey Of An Outsider" (R J W Selleck, Woburn Press, Ilford, 1994).

His eldest brother, Captain Lawrence Kay-Shuttleworth, was killed on Friday 30th March 1917 and is buried in Villers Station Cemetery, Villers-au-Bois.

Lawrence Kay-Shuttleworth

THE MOST REVEREND AND RIGHT HONOURABLE COSMO GORDON LANG, GCVO, PC, DD
1ST BARON LANG OF LAMBETH
The Archbishop of York

Cosmo Lang and the coat of arms of the Sees of Canterbury and York

Cosmo was born in Fyvie, Aberdeenshire, on Monday 31st October 1864, son of the Very Reverend John Marshall Lang, CVO, DD, LLD, Principal of Aberdeen University and Mrs Hannah Agnes Lang. He was educated at the Park School and went up to Glasgow University followed by Balliol College, Oxford.

Cosmo was ordained a Deacon in 1890, a Priest in 1891, Curate of Leeds from 1890 to 1893, Examination Chaplain to the Bishop of Lichfield 1893 to 1895, Vicar of St Mary, Oxford, 1894 to 1896, Examination Chaplain to the Bishop of Oxford 1894 to 1901, Honorary Chaplain to HM Queen Victoria 1899 to 1901, Vicar of Portsea, Hampshire and Chaplain of Kingston Prison 1896 to 1901, Canon Residentiary and Treasurer of St Paul's Cathedral 1901 to 1909, Bishop of Stepney in 1901 and Archbishop of York in 1909.

On Tuesday 4th December 1928 Cosmo was enthroned as Archbishop of Canterbury. He was closely involved in the Abdication Crisis and did not support HM King Edward VIII. He crowned HM King George VI in Westminster Abbey on Wednesday 12th May 1937. He retired on Tuesday

31st March 1942, one of his last official duties being the confirmation of HRH Princess Elizabeth (HM Queen Elizabeth II) three days previously. He was created Baron Lang of Lambeth and lived until Wednesday 5th December 1945.
Cosmo was the Chaplain and Prelate of the Order of St John of Jerusalem.

DAVID LLOYD GEORGE
1ST EARL LLOYD-GEORGE OF DWYFOR

Lloyd-George and his coat of arms

Lloyd George was born in Chortlon-on-Medlock on Saturday 17th January 1863, son of William and Elizabeth. After school he studied the law and became a solicitor in 1885. He married Margaret Owen on Tuesday 24th January 1888 and the next year was appointed an Alderman on Caenarfonshire County Council. He was elected as a Liberal Member of Parliament for Caernarfon Borough at a by-election on Monday 13th April 1890, remaining in the House until 1945. He joined Sir Henry Campbell-Bannerman's Government in 1906 as President of the Board of Trade. From 1908 to 1915 he was the Chancellor of the Exchequer. He was appointed Minister of Munitions in 1915, followed by the Secretary State for War in 1916 before he became Prime Minister. He continued to serve as Prime Minister until 1922 and finally fell when it became clear that he was selling honours. From 1929 to 1945 he was the Father of the House. In March 1936 he met Adolf Hitler at Berchtesgarten whom he described as "the greatest living German". His wife died on Monday 20th January 1941 and he married his long-time mistress, Frances Stevenson. He was elevated to the peerage as the 1st Earl on Monday 1st January 1945, however, died on Monday 26th March without ever taking his seat in the House.

Lloyd George speaking in 1917

Personalities In The Text

Lieutenant Ian Maclean Macandrew
1st Battalion Seaforth Highlanders
Died on Wednesday 23rd December 1914, aged 23
Commemorated on Panel 38, Le Touret Memorial.

Ian Macandrew

Ian was born at East Haugh, Perthshire, on Friday 30th October 1891, the only son of Major J Maclean Macandrew (3rd Seaforth Highlanders) and Mrs Elsie Mabel Macandrew, of Delniesmuir, Nairn, and grandson of Major General W Lambert Yonge, RA. He was educated at Winchester College from 1905 to 1910 where he was an exhibitioner and won the King's silver medal for Latin Speech. Ian was a good athlete playing in the XV as well as winning a number of cups for running from the hundred yards to the quarter-mile. He went up to New College Oxford where he graduated with a BA in History in June 1913. Ian's main interest were all country pursuits and he was a good shot; he was a member of the Junior United Service Club.

Ian was gazetted to the Seaforths and joined the 1st Battalion in Agra, India. Following the outbreak of war he sailed to Marseilles and was promoted to Lieutenant in September 1914. He was wounded on Friday 6th November however chose to return to the front line rather be hospitalised. He was leading his men in action at Festubert when the trenches to their left were abandoned. Ian rallied all the men around him and managed to hold the line, however, in the action he was killed.

Ian was Mentioned in Despatches on Thursday 14th January 1915.

Festubert village

... a dressing station

Personalities In The Text

Brigadier General
Ronald Campbell Maclachlan, DSO
General Staff, Commanding 112th Infantry Brigade, Rifle Brigade
Died on Saturday 11th August 1917, aged 45
Grave reference II. C. 9, Locre Hospice Cemetery

Citation for the Distinguished Service Order, London Gazette, Saturday 3rd June 1916:
"War Office, 3 June 1916. His Majesty the King has been graciously pleased to approve of the undermentioned rewards for distinguished service in the field." His name is listed below.

Ronald was born on Wednesday 24th July 1872, fourth son of the Reverend Archibald Neil Campbell Maclachlan, of Newton Valence, Alton, Hampshire. He was educated at Eton College as a member of Mr Francis Warre Cornish's House, leaving in 1891 and passed into RMC Sandhurst. Ronald married Elinor Mary Maclachlan (daughter of Mr J C Cox, MP), of Rookley House, Kings Somborne, Hampshire.

Ronald was gazetted on Saturday 8th July 1893, promoted to Lieutenant on Wednesday 27th November 1895, Captain on Tuesday 24th April 1900, Major on Wednesday 26th January 1910.

Ronald served in India with the 3rd Battalion and during the South African War he served with the 2nd Battalion, where he was severely wounded at Wagon Hill on Saturday 6th January 1900. He was Mentioned in Despatches on Tuesday 10th September 1901 for work with his machine guns, and received the Queen's Medal with three clasps. After the war he returned to India and took part in the Tibet Expedition on 1903 and 1904 where he received the Medal. From Saturday 1st February 1908 to Saturday 30th September 1911 he was appointed Adjutant of the OTC in Oxford, and was rewarded with an Honorary MA from Oxford University when he relinquished his post.

In June 1914 Ronald was appointed Commander of the Oxford OTC and promoted Lieutenant Colonel. At the outbreak of war he was with his men in Camp at Churn. He then assisted in raising and training the 8th Battalion and took it out to France in 1915 and was promoted Temporary Brigadier General. He was severely wounded on Monday 20th December 1915. He was gazetted Brigadier General on Sunday 7th January 1917. He fought through the Battle of Arras, and at Monchy-le-Preux, his Divisional General wrote of him: *"We wondered how it was possible for the Germans to have let his men get to the summit of the ridge where there was not a blade of cover. It was his personal example and personal influence only that did it. He was right up to the front, almost in the front line."*

Ronald was killed by a sniper about 7.00am whilst touring with the front with Lieutenant Colonel Dill in the Oosttaverne Sector.

Personalities In The Text

It was written of him: *"In his Regiment he was beloved, and the large number who attended his funeral was eloquent testimony of the esteem in which he was held by all. But his influence counts much further than his Regiment, and there must be almost hundreds of Oxford men who are under a great obligation to him for having taught them the duties of an officer."*

As a Lieutenant-Colonel, he wrote to the Grenfell parents, Lord and Lady Desborough, on each occasion after the death of their sons.

On the mid-outer wall on the north aisle in Winchester Cathedral, Hampshire an elaborate stone tablet was raised with a carved wreath painted green and inscribed: *"This tablet is placed by his wife in honoured memory of Brigadier General Ronald Campbell Maclachlan, D.S.O., the Rifle Brigade, who fell in action Aug. 11. 1917 near Locre in The Great European War."*

A white marble tablet and a stained glassed window were erected as a MacLachlan Family Memorial in St Mary The Blessed Virgin Church, Newton Valence, Hampshire: *"In honour of the warrior Saints George & Martin & in thankful remembrance of three soldier brothers Neil, Major Seaforth Highlanders who fell in India May 24th 1908 & Ronald, Brigadier General Rifle Brigade D.S.O. killed in action in France Aug. 11th 1917 and Alexander Fraser, Lieutenant Colonel King's Royal Rifles D.S.O. killed in action in France March 22nd 1918. These two windows are dedicated by their brother Archibald Campbell Maclachlan and his sisters Mary Abigail & Eveleen. Anno Domini 1919 "Fortis Et Fidus"*

Left window: *"Here Saint George Slayeth The Loathly Beast 'Sanctus Georgius'."*

Right window: *"Here St Michael Divideth His Cloak With The Beggar' 'Sanctus Martinus."*

His brother, Lieutenant Colonel Alexander Maclachlan, DSO, died on Friday 22nd March 1918 and is buried in Savy British Cemetery.

John Gordon Swift MacNeill, KC, MP

Swift was born on Sunday 11th March 1849, the only son of the Reverend John Gordon Swift MacNeill and his wife Susan and as related to Jonathan Swift. He went up to Trinity College, Dublin, followed by Christ Church, Oxford. In 1875 he was called to the Irish Bar, appointed a QC in 1893 and was a Professor of Law at King's Inn followed by that National University of Ireland. He was elected at a by-election in 1887 as the Member of Parliament for South Donegal, as a Protestant Nationalist, and continued to represent the constituency until 1918 when he was deselected.

Swift died on Thursday 24th August 1926.

PERSONALITIES IN THE TEXT

WALTER TURNER MONCKTON
1ST VISCOUNT MONCKTON OF BRENCHLEY, GCVO, KCMG

Walter was born on Saturday 17th January 1891 in Plaxtol, Kent. He was educated at Harrow School and went up to Balliol College, Oxford, where he excelled at cricket — later in life becoming the President of the MCC and Surrey County Cricket Club.

During the First World War he served with the Royal West Kent Regiment and was awarded the Military Cross.

Walter Monckton

Walter studied law and later became Attorney-General to the Duchy of Cornwall and continued to advise King Edward VIII, including during the abdication crisis.

In 1951 he was elected as a Member of Parliament for Bristol West being appointed Minister of Labour and National Service under Churchill, followed by Minister of Defence and Paymaster-General under Eden. In 1957 he was raised to the peerage and was appointed Lord Chief Justice. Walter Monckton died on Saturday 9th January 1965.

SECOND LIEUTENANT THOMAS KEITH HEDLEY RAE
'C' Company, 8th Battalion Rifle Brigade
Died on Friday 30th July 1915, aged 25
Commemorated on Panel 46, The Menin Gate.

Keith was born at home on Wednesday 24th May 1899, third and youngest son of Edward and Margaret Rae, of Courthill, Birkenhead. He was educated privately due to ill-health as a child and adolescent. He went up to Balliol College, Oxford, in 1907, graduating in 1912 with a Second in History. Keith was a friend of Gilbert Talbot. Thomas established a Boys' Club in Oxford that continued long after his death and worked with Ronald Poulton-Palmer and Stephen Reiss (who are buried in Hyde Park Corner (Royal Berks) Cemetery and commemorated on the Loos Memorial respectively). He played for the College Hockey XI. After coming down from Balliol Thomas was employed as an Assistant Master at Marlborough College

Keith Rae

teaching English. In 1913 he visited Germany to study German.
At the outbreak of war Keith volunteered and was commissioned in December 1914. He trained at Aldershot, leaving for Boulogne on Wednesday 19th May 1915. Upon arrival the Battalion entrained to Watten where they camped.
Keith was sent across the border into Belgium and took the line for the first time on

Monday 7th June in front of St Eloi. On Thursday 22nd July the British blew a mine at Hooge, however, failed to fully capitalise on it, two days later the Germans blew one of their own. The Germans had lost ground and it was clear that a counter-attack would be launched. The German infantry moved forward with their special back-packs filled with inflammable liquid, and pouring forth their crimson fire and black smoke. It was a terrifying sight and the attack forced the British defenders back. Keith was killed in action whilst standing on the parapet of his trench in front of Hooge Château, despite being severely burnt he continued to resist the German attack. He was described as being seen shortly before he died: " ... *burnt and bleeding, standing on his parapet firing at the attackers."*

His parents erected the monument on the spot they believed him to have been killed near Hooge Château. Baron de Vinck asked for the memorial to be removed as he could not continue to maintain it, in 1966 it was moved to just outside Sanctuary Wood Cemetery. The memorial, in the form of a Celtic cross is based on the one at Marlborough College (upon which he is also commemorated.

The Memorial is inscribed:

On the plinth: *"In memory of Keith Rae, 2 Lt. 8th Rifle Brigade, dearest loved younger son of Edward and Margaret Rae, who died on this spot 30th July 1915 in his 25th year fighting in The Great War for humanity."*

On the base: *"Be thee faithful unto death I will give thee a crown of life."*

On the front: *"'In memory also of his brother officers and men who fell on the same morning and afternoon."*

On the rear: *"This monument originally erected beside Hooge Crater and dedicated on 15th May 1921 was transferred to this site in 1966."*

A plaque, now held in Balliol College Dean's Office, was originally in the Boys' Club Sports Pavilion that was demolished for redevelopment: *"Keith Rae House built in memory of Keith Rae, President of the years 1909-10 of the Balliol College Boys' Club. 2nd Lieut., 8th Battalion the Rifle Brigade, he was killed at dawn on 30th July 1915 defending his trench at Hooghe, Les Ypres, when the Germans first attacked with liquid fire. Christ's faithful soldier and servant unto his life's end."*

In St Saviours Church, Bidston, Oxton, Merseyside, a wood panel was placed behind the altar in his memory with the inscription: *"In memory of Keith Rae 2nd Lieut. 8th Btn. Rifle Brig. and the very dearly loved youngest son of Edward & Margaret Rae. He died fighting at Hooghe Les Ypres 30th July 1915 in his 27th year. Christ's faithful soldier and servant unto his life's end."*

Keith is also commemorated on the War Memorial at the Royal Liverpool Golf Club, Hoylake. A bequest was made to establish an Exhibition for a Balliol entrant at Marlborough College.

PERSONALITIES IN THE TEXT

SECOND LIEUTENANT SIDNEY CLAYTON WOODROFFE, VC
8th Battalion Rifle Brigade
Died on Friday 30th July 1915, aged 19
Commemorated on Panel 46, The Menin Gate.

Citation for the Victoria Cross, London Gazette No 29286, dated Friday 3rd September 1915:

"For most conspicuous bravery on 30th July, 1915, at Hooge. The enemy having broken through the centre of our front trenches, consequent on the use of burning liquids, this Officer's position was heavily attacked with bombs from the flank and subsequently from the rear, but he managed to defend his post until all his bombs were exhausted, and then skilfully withdrew his remaining men. This very gallant Officer immediately led his party forward in a counter-attack under an intense rifle and machine-gun fire, and was killed whilst in the act of cutting the wire obstacles in the open."

Sidney Woodroffe

Sidney was born in Lewes on Tuesday 17th December 1895, the fourth and youngest son of Henry and Clara Woodroffe, of Branksome Avenue, Bournemouth. He was educated at Marlborough College where he was Senior Prefect, Captain of the OTC, played for the Rugby XV, Hockey XI and Cricket XI. He went up to Pembroke College, Cambridge, with a Classical Scholarship, in 1911.

Sidney was gazetted a 2nd Lieutenant in the 8th Battalion Rifle Brigade on Wednesday 23rd December 1914 and was sent to join the Battalion at Aldershot. He continued training with the men until leaving for Boulogne on Wednesday 19th May 1915. He was sent to continue his training at Watten; on Friday 28th he was attached to the Staffordshires for a week's training to become accustomed with front line life and duties. Two days after the completion of his training Sidney took his men into the line on their first tour of duty in front of St Eloi that lasted for three days. The tedium of 'normal' tours of duties continued for the next four weeks.

Whilst in the front line the Germans laid a barrage on their line on Monday 5th July and followed it up with a raid. In short order the front line trench was compromised, and a party of twenty Germans were in their trenches. Lieutenant Backus had been buried alive during the barrage however was successfully dug out. He then led the men, together with the bombing officer of the North Staffordshires, to drive out the Germans at the point of the bayonet and with the bomb. Trench life continued to normality with tours of duty alternating by days of relief and training.

Lieutenant Colonel Ronald Maclachlan (see above) wrote: *"Your younger boy was simply one of the bravest of the brave; later I will try to get you a more or less definite*

Personalities In The Text

account. When the line was attacked and broken on his right he still held his trench, and only when the Germans were discovered to be in rear of him did he leave it. He then withdrew his remaining men very skilfully right away to a flank and worked his way alone back to me to report. He finally brought his command back and then took part in the counter-attack. He was killed out in front, in the open, cutting the wire to enable the attack to be continued. This is the bald statement of his part of that day's action. He risked his life for others right through the day and finally gave it for the sake of his men. He was a splendid type of young officer, always bold as a lion, confident and sure of himself too. The loss he is to me personally is very great, as I have learnt to appreciate what a sterling fine lad he was. His men would have followed him anywhere."

His brothers, Lieutenant Kenneth Woodroffe, died on Sunday 9th May 1915 and is commemorated on the Le Touret Memorial and Captain Leslie Woodroffe, died on Sunday 4th June 1916 and is buried in Barlin Communal Cemetery Extension.

... the attackers bomb their way forward

TOC H AND TALBOT HOUSE

"All rank abandon, ye who enter here".

The Reverend Phillip Thomas Byard Clayton, an Army Chaplain known as *'Tubby'* opened a club and rest house for the soldiers, *'Everyman's Club'* at 43 Gasthuisstraat, Poperinghe on 11th December 1915. He was supported by a fellow Chaplain, Neville Talbot, the brother of Lieutenant Gilbert Talbot who had been a friend of *'Tubby'*. It was decided that the house would be renamed *'Talbot House'* in Gilbert's memory and TOC H came from the signallers code of T (TOC) and H (H).

The house was furnished with gifts, including a piano, and soon parcels of books and assorted paraphernalia were arriving from England to supplement their stocks. The loft was converted into a chapel and became known as *'The Upper Room'* that remains as it was during the war and can be visited. It is here that Gilbert's original battlefield cross is now displayed.

'Tubby's' creation soon became very popular with the troops that visited Poperinghe on rest periods and it was continuously crowded. In 1916 part of an adjacent hop store was acquired that became *'The Concert Hall'*.

Following the end of the First World War the property was reoccupied by its original owner, Mr Coevoet Camerlynck. In the early 1920s veterans of the war came to revisit their old battlefields and during the Pilgrimages large numbers would call at their much-loved Talbot House. In 1929 Mr Camerlynck sold the property to Lord Wakefield of Hythe for £9,200 who immediately donated it to TOC H.

TUBBY CLAYTON

'Tubby' Clayton was born in Queensland, Australia, on Saturday 12th December 1885, returning with his parents to England two years later. He was educated at St Paul's School and Exeter College, Oxford. He was ordained and became the curate of St Mary's Church, Portsea, from 1910 to 1915. He became an Army Chaplain in early 1915 and went out to France and Belgium.

When he returned to England after the war he continued his work with the TOC H movement. He was appointed vicar of All Hallows-by-the-Tower in 1922 and remained there for forty years. *'Tubby'* died in December 1972.

'Tubby' Clayton

Gilbert Walter Lyttelton Talbot

To Arms!

Books covering the First World War cemeteries and war memorials:

'In Continuing and Grateful Memory'

Belgium
Beyond the Salient
Lijssenthoek Military Cemetery
The Menin Gate
The Ploegsteert Sector
The Ypres Salient
Tyne Cot Cemetery and Memorial

France
Arras Memorial, Arras Flying Memorial and Faubourg d'Amiens Cemetery
Le Touret Memorial and Le Touret Military Cemetery, Richebourg-l'Avoue
Loos Memorial
Thiepval Memorial
Cemeteries by Department (individual sets of books)

Europe
Balkans
England
Gallipoli and Turkey
Germany and the Netherlands
Helles Memorial
Iberian Peninsula and the Mediterranean
Italy
Northern Europe (Baltic States, Poland, Russia and Scandinavia)
Scotland
The Naval Memorials of Chatham, Plymouth, Portsmouth and Merchant Naval Memorial (Tower Bridge)
Wales

Other Sectors
Africa
Australasia
Egypt and North Africa
Iraq and Iran
The Americas
The Indian Subcontinent
The Palestinian Campaign

In continuing & Grateful Memory
Specialised Battlefield Tours

I began organising battlefield tours to the Western Front in 1981. In the early years I enjoyed taking veterans back to where they had served on the battlefields, from Ypres to the Somme. Many of them had never previously returned to the battlefields they had left at the end of the First World War — sadly those opportunities no longer exist.

The fully-guided specialised tours normally are for four or five days. We stay in a high standard of hotels (based in central locations), with all meals, museum entrances *et al* included. (The only additional costs are for personal drinks and single room supplements.) The tours welcome everyone and we provide time to accommodate individual requests and visits. We cater for all levels of knowledge — from the expert to the first-time visitor.

The main aim is that you enjoy your trip; also that you will improve your knowledge, visit new places, return feeling you have received good value for money — then come back again on another tour!

Each year a tour Ypres for 11th November has become an institution which includes, in addition to tour of the Salient and the ceremonies in the town, a Remembrance Day Reception and Dinner with an after-dinner speech. The tours throughout the rest of the year are based on specific battles, places and personalities with new tours added each year. An full information pack with notes and maps support the tour.

If you would be interested in joining a forthcoming tour and would like further information please contact me:

visit: www.remembering1418.com

email: remembering@btinternet.com

post: c/o 15 Cress Way, Faversham, Kent ME13 7NH

I look forward to the opportunity of meeting you on a tour.

Paul Foster